Introduction To The BYNV
BESORAH OF YAHUSHA NATSARIM VERSION

Lew White
Copyright © 2019

ALSO AVAILABLE AS KINDLE BOOK
AT LEW WHITE'S AUTHOR'S PAGE

This Is The Way, Walk In It

CONTENTS - WHAT'S INSIDE

3	ABOUT THE COVER
4	FOREWORD
6	INTRODUCTION TO THE BYNV TRANSLATION
29	Taking Scripture At Its Word Isn't Popular
46	WHAT DO THE FESTIVALS MEAN?
53	MESSAGE OF ALIYAHU
53	WHAT IS HIS NAME? (SEE ALSO PAGE 74)
56	NIV & NASB - IN THEIR OWN WORDS
66	JESUIT INTERVIEWS ONE OF THE NATSARIM
81	GLOSSARY
93	HOW TO GRAFT-IN
111	LOVE DEFINED
113	LETTER CHART

ABOUT THE COVER

The word "LOVE" is spelled by the position of the arms of the figures on the front cover. This form of sign-messaging is called semaphore. The message of love is signaling to every person who has eyes to see and hear it. The everlasting arms of love are calling to every heart to be restored to love.
A prophet foretold this message would be startling:

"Yahuah shall lay bare His qodesh arm in the eyes of all the guyim. And all the ends of the arets shall see the deliverance of our Alahim. Turn aside! Turn aside! Come out from there, touch not the unclean. Come out of her midst, be clean, you who bear the vessels of Yahuah. For you shall not come out in haste, nor go in flight. For Yahuah is going before you, and the Alahim of Yisharal is your rear guard. See, My Servant shall work wisely, He shall be exalted and lifted up and very high. As many were astonished at You – so the disfigurement beyond any man's and His form beyond the sons of men – He shall likewise startle many guyim."
(YashaYahu / Isaiah 52:10-15 BYNV)
See Glossary for understanding unfamilar words

FOREWORD

There's a new awakening taking place all over the Earth. Yahusha is pouring-out His breath into the minds of many people to prepare them for His return to reign. The lies of the dragon are being exposed, and crowds are abandoning the false teachings handed-down over generations. The true followers of Yahusha are called Natsarim (YirmeYahu / Jeremiah 31:6, Acts 24:5), and we are abiding in His Word, going against the advice of the false teachers.
Their programming to disregard the Commandments is no longer working, and they are exhibiting the rage of their true master.

Obedience Enrages The Dragon

Teachers of traditions are becoming very disturbed because people are now breaking free of their bonds. We are multiplying all over the Earth with the true message of repent, or perish. One cannot disobey the Ten Commandments of love, and then claim they know Yahusha (1 Yn. 2:4-6).

The dragon has hidden Yahusha's Name, and caused lawlessness to increase, while using the wealth of those they are deceiving to perpetuate the lies our fathers have inherited. Obedience is the evidence of what we believe, and who we are the servants of (Romans 6:16). Without obedience, our belief is dead. Join us. We are the last Natsarim, and we teach the Name and the Word, enraging the dragon (Rev. 12:17). We pursue lawfulness, and are called legalists. This is exactly what Yahusha wants all of us to be (Ecclesiastes 12:1-14). There is no way to live illegally, and say Yahusha is pleased with us.

Look carefully at the fruit, and you can identify the tree.

"I am the Vine, you are the Natsarim."

The Covenant of kindness (asereth ha dabarim, 10 words) is our marriage covenant with our Husband, Yahusha. Without living in them, mankind languishes, never learning how to love. They are prominently shown on the back cover, and are to be posted on our doorposts and gates. Commit them to memory, guard them, and teach them.
A king of Yisharal who love them dearly once said,

"How would a young man cleanse his path. To guard it according to Your Word? I have sought You with all my heart; Let me not stray from Your commands! I have treasured up Your Word in my heart, that I might not sin against You. Blessed are You, O Yahuah! Teach me Your laws. With my lips I have recounted All the directives of Your mouth. I have rejoiced in the way of Your witnesses, As over all riches. I meditate on Your orders, and regard Your ways. I delight myself in Your laws; I do not forget Your Word. Do good to Your servant, Let me live and I guard Your word. Open my eyes, that I might see Wonders from Your Turah."
(Psalm 119:9-18 BYNV)

The branches that abide in His Word will not be dry, but green because He is in them bearing His fruits.
www.fossilizedcustoms.com/natsarim.html

INTRODUCTION TO THE BYNV TRANSLATION
AVAILABLE INSTANTLY AS AN E-BOOK FROM AMAZON

INTRODUCTION TO THE BYNV

The WORD of Yahuah is one Person. As He spoke through the prophets, He uses the first and last letters of the Hebrew alef-beth (alphabet) in specific locations throughout the **TaNaK** to identify Himself as the One that is speaking. These two letters remain a mystery to translators, who generally ignore them and what they mean. Some believe they should be understood as part of the syntax of the sentences, operating as modifiers. These two letters are not "et", but rather "at," **alef-tau**. The revelation of their meaning is provided at the beginning and ending of this book, called "Revelation." The letters mark His Words so we would make the connection to Him. These 2 letters are identity marks of the One speaking. All the time it's been Him, the One Who said He would be with us, and to be strong and courageous. Be still, and know that He is Alahim.

8ᵀᴴ CENTURY MASORETES (A KARAITE SECT)

Jeho, Yeho, or Yahu?

A Karaite sect called the **Masoretes** (8th – 11th century "tradition-keepers") invented vowel points to guide all Yahudim in the uniform pronunciation of Hebrew words. This man-made system secured one major objective: to keep the pronunciation of the Name, **Yahuah**, from **everyone's** lips. There are not such marks found on any of the Dead Sea Scrolls. The invented niqqud marks were added in the 8th century. Yahusha is in His Natsarim, and He reveals the Name, and reveals the secrets that have been invented by men to keep it held back. Many of our strongholds involve human traditions, and there are many more strongholds we must overthrow. The **key of knowledge** that has been withheld in other versions is being revealed again, shown on the **stone** and **coin** below. It is the **Name "turning the world upside down"** (Acts 17:6).

"YAHU"
PERSIAN COIN IN CAPTIVES' DISTRICT

ARCH OF TITUS SHOWING MENORAH

This kindle translation **transliterates** many original Hebrew words. The Name of the Creator appears in English letters: **Yahuah, Yahusha** At Exodus 31:18 we learn that on Mount Sinai the Creator engraved two stone tablets with His finger, and gave them to Mushah (Moses). He engraved His Name using four ancient vowels, in Hebrew letters:
Yod-Hay-Uau-Hay

The four vowels of YHUH are often represented by the Latin letters **YHWH**. In their original form they appeared as the letters in stone found in Shamarun pictured above. This is the script used by the Creator of the universe. Stones cry out this

Name. **Yahuah** used men to write His message to mankind in ancient (palaeo), primary Hebrew. The ancient (palaeo) Hebrew letters sound the same, although they look drastically different from the modern Babylonian script commonly seen today. YashaYahu (Isaiah) 34:16 admonishes us to seek the book/scroll of **Yahuah**, and in that scroll we find **Yahuah**'s Name written in the ancient (palaeo), primary Hebrew. How did we come to embrace the Babylonian script (modern Hebrew)? The **House of Yahudah** was taken captive to Babylon around 586 BCE. Upon their release after 70 years, they brought back the Babylonian letter shapes which we now refer to as "modern Hebrew." About half the book of Danial (one of the Babylonian captives) is written in the original Hebrew, and the rest in the Babylonian script, Aramaic. Danial was able to read the "old" script used by Yahuah when the handwriting on the wall appeared, but the Babylonians could not [see Danial 5]. As scrolls would wear-out, the scribes copied the scrolls in the newer Babylonian letter shapes for the general text, but the Name Yahuah was preserved in the original form. When they came to the Name, they carefully preserved the palaeo-Hebrew form in its authentic form. This word is used at least 6,823 times in the TaNaK. **TaNaK** is an acronym for Turah, Nabi'im, and Kethubim, or the Instructions, the Prophets, and the Writings. We also know that the earliest copies of the Septuagint (LXX) translation into Greek preserved the palaeo-Hebrew for **Yahuah**'s Name, whereas later copies used the Greek word *Kurios* (Lord) to replace it. By replacing it, they wiped it out. The Greek word **THEOS** (deity) produces *invented terms* such as **GOD** and "**godhead**."

THE SEPTUAGINT, OR LXX
The LXX transliterated the spelling of **Yahusha** (KJV: Joshua) into the Greek letters **IESOUS** for the successor of Mushah. Those who rely on this as evidence that it is acceptable to allow the Greek form to define the original Hebrew are simply

moving the error further into the past, and not recognizing it as a corruption. This is a method of deception called *casuistry*. The Greek alphabet is unable to convey the correct sounds of certain Hebrew letters because it has no "SH" sound, and no letter "Y." The third commandment in Exodus 20:7 says we are not to *shoah* (destroy) His Name, or cast it to ruin. Yet, by denying or avoiding **Yahuah**'s Name and the Name of His Son Yahusha, both Judaism and Christianity have done exactly that, breaking the third commandment.

While in Babylon, the House of Yahudah was enslaved. They heard the Babylonians using the Name in disrespectful ways, profaning it. To help prevent this from happening, those in leadership put into effect a ban against pronouncing **Yahuah**'s Name, declaring it to be **ineffable**. By never saying the Name, it quickly became unknown to even the Yahudim. This ban is completely contrary to Scripture. **Yahuah** commands us over and over again in Scripture to utter, proclaim, and **lift up** His authentic Hebrew Name. It's of paramount importance to understand that if we continue to use counterfeit names or devices for the Father and His Son, we will not be in true worship nor truly know the One we serve; we will leave ourselves open for the enemy to step in as the author of confusion, and we will be deceived. Yahusha mentioned that they had **"taken away the key of knowledge"** (Luke 11:52), but He was restoring it again. We find in Genesis 4:26 that **Yahuah**'s Name began to be called upon, and continued to be called upon up to and during the first Temple period. When the House of Yahudah was taken captive to Babylon, the pagan Babylonian influences took a firm grip on their hearts and minds. In our modern translations, we see the result of this ban of ineffability in the fact that **Yahuah**'s Name has been entirely omitted, and replaced with titles, or terms which can apply to any Pagan deity, almost seven thousand times. Because the ineffability of the Name is not sound doctrine, the new translation you are holding restores our Father's Name and that of His Son by using the original palaeo-Hebrew script. It is found on the "Great Isaiah Scroll" among the Dead Sea Scrolls, which is now on display in the Shrine of the Book. Many ancient artifacts prove its authenticity, such as ostracons, seals, lamps, stone reliefs, and coins. By replacing the true Name into the text as it was originally written, we have done what has not been done since the first translation was made in the 2nd century BCE. That first translation from Hebrew to Greek has been named the **Septuagint**, and is abbreviated with the Latin letters for seventy: **LXX**.

RABBINICAL JUDAISM
(concerns teachings, not people): Proverbs 30:4 asks us a weighty question, "...What is His Name, and what is His Son's Name..." Rabbinical Judaism, the leaven / teachings of the Pharisees, calls **Yahuah** by the substitute terms, "HaShem, Adonai or Alahim" - none of which are His Name; they are titles or pronouns. Christians use "Jehovah" for the Father and "Jesus" for the Son, both of which are not authentic; they are imprinted with the corruptions found in the Greek and Latin alphabets. The Names can't be "Jehovah" or "Jesus", because there is no letter "**J**" in Hebrew (the letter "J" appeared on Earth during the 16th century). The Greek language added the ending letter S to the Name of Yahusha.

ORIGIN OF WORD "GOD"
We discover that Yahuah removed His Name from our lips during the captivity in Babel [see YirmeYahu 44:26]. The device "**LORD**" has been embraced to refer to Yahuah. Another term, **GOD**, has come to replace the original Hebrew word "Alahim." Read Exodus 23:13 right now. With that Scripture in mind, consider the following reference: The **Encyclopedia Americana** (1945 Edition) says under the topic **GOD**: **GOD** (god); **"Common Teutonic word for personal object of religious worship, formerly applicable to super-**

human beings of heathen myth; on conversion of Teutonic races to Christianity, term was applied to Supreme Being." 1 Thessalonians 5:22 warns us not to give the appearance of evil, and this would have to include what comes from our mouths. Guile is deceit. When we speak guile using replacement names, or use titles in place of His Name, we are breaking the third commandment and giving the appearance of evil in our speech. We are **circumlocuting** *(talking around)* the Name, but not really saying it. *"He knows who we mean"* is the common response. Many say they don't use the Name because they want to keep from offending people. They don't mind offending Yahuah; He knows *their heart.* Or they say, "We speak English, not Hebrew." Why do they get upset with the Name Yahusha, and not Abraham, Adam, or the many other Hebrew names? It is because would have to admit their programming is flawed, and they desire to hold on to it more than they desire to receive the Truth, understand, and turn away from their former teaching authority. Their logic is controlled by the sophistry of their teachers. Ask anyone if they know the name of the ruler of Babel that took away the house of Yahudah, destroyed the first Temple, and they will tell you it was "**Nebuchadnetsar**." They deny being able to speak Hebrew, yet they can clearly pronounce many names written in Scripture, except the one Name they deny being able to say.

LORD IN HEBREW IS BEL?
Numbers 6:24-27 reveals **Yahuah**'s Name will be upon His people: What Name would that be, the **LORD**? Again, in Genesis 4:26 we learn that men began to call upon **Yahuah**'s Name. There is only one Name given under heaven (Acts 4:12). In 1 Kings 18:24 we find that Aliyahu (Elijah) called on the Name of **Yahuah** while the pagans called on the names of their deities (Bel and Asherah); clearly there must be a distinction in what we call our Creator. "**Bel**" in Hebrew means "**lord.**" It follows that LORD is not the true name we should be

calling upon. Deuteronomy 28:10 reveals that all Guyim will see that we are called by **Yahuah**'s **Name.** Revelation 22:4 tells us His people will be sealed with **Yahuah**'s Name in their foreheads. Malaki 3:16 commands us to think upon **Yahuah**'s Name, but historically neither Judaism nor the *Kirche* have been thinking on His true Hebrew Name. Micah 4:5 reveals that we are to walk in **Yahuah**'s Name. Psalms 83:16-18 **Yahuah** commands us to seek His Name. Psalms 72:17 tells us that **Yahuah**'s Name will endure forever, but Judaism and the Kurk (Kirke, or Circus, the original term for a pagan place of worship) have placed a stumbling block where His Name is concerned. Not only have they both forgotten His Name but they have "destroyed" **Yahuah**'s Name thousands and thousands of times in Scripture. The Hebrew term for the "called-out" is the QAHAL, and today we think of the assembly, as well as a meeting place, as a "kurche" - **KIRKE**, the **Greek** term for a pagan Temple, and derived from the name of a witch, **CIRCE,** sometimes rendered "KIRCHE" in English. Regarding praise and worship, we are told in 2 Samuel 7:26 that we are to magnify **Yahuah**'s Name, but in reality we have been magnifying unscriptural names and mere titles that might apply to any generic, non-specific deity. Psalms 106:47 says that we are to give thanksgiving to **Yahuah**'s Name, but clearly we've been giving thanksgiving to foreign names. Psalms 29:2 says we are to esteem **Yahuah**'s Name. Psalms 9:2 says that we are to sing praises to **Yahuah**'s Name. YashaYahu (Isaiah) 56:6 reveals that we are to **love Yahuah**'s Name. Psalms 45:17 says every generation is to remember **Yahuah**'s Name. Exodus 3:14,15 teaches His memorial Name to all generations is: **Yahuah. How can we remember what we've never heard? Our teachers have led us into confusion. It's time to wake up.** Deliverance is found in **Yahuah**'s Name and that of His Son, Yahusha, Psalms 54:1; Joel 2:32 and Acts 2:21; 4:12. Clearly, we are to call on **Yahuah**'s Name and the Name of His Son for deliverance. Are we to use counterfeit names or common titles when we pray for redemption? Using a personal name is a matter of *identification.* Pronouncing a person's name as well as we can is a sign of respectfulness and consideration. Men have hidden, disguised, corrupted, and substituted the Name if our Creator. "Jehovah" and "Jesus" are of recent origin. They say, "We don't speak Hebrew," yet they only have a problem with one Hebrew word – His NAME. Hebrew words are used for people, places, and greetings all the time. Some examples are Abraham, shalom, Bethlehem, Adam, Michael, Aaron, Abel, Abilene, Abner, Denmark, London, Daniel, and around 50,000 Hebrew (Eberith) words people have no idea are used in the English language. Even our Latin alphabet traces directly from the Greek letters, derived from Hebrew.

THE NAME JEHOVAH

Instead of Jehovah, the Name appeared as **Iehoua** in the *Geneva translation*, and in the first printings of the KJV. In subsequent printings of the KJV, the letter J began to be used for the first letter of proper nouns that began with the letter I, and at the beginning of sentences. The letter J is but a few hundred years old. What's startling though is this: when Jehovah is broken down we have "Je hovah" with the "Je" replacing His shortened, poetic name "Yah." "HOVAH" is referenced in **Strong's Exhaustive Concordance** as word H1943, and means lay-waste, destruction, or ruin. When we speak the hybrid name "Je**hovah**", we are in essence saying "Yah, He is ruin." This idea is the result of people mixing roots improperly. Written letters changed their sounds over recent centuries. The letter shaped "V" we see used over 400 years ago is the old Latin shape that functioned as our modern letter U. The Latin word GLADIVS in its old form utilizes the V-SHAPE, but it SOUNDED like our modern letter U. Because of this distortion, the spelling JEHOVAH has been misunderstood by today's reader. To correctly understand the pronunciation, the J sounds like a Y, and the V sounds like a U. The "OU" (or "OV") is simply a diphthong, making the word really sound like "Ya-Hoo-ah", so the *ovah* portion would be improved for today by writing it *ouah*. This produces Yah+ *ouah*. The transliteration (trans-lettering) of many words and names is being better understood when these obstacles are removed. An early transliteration of the Name Yahuah into Greek used the letters **IAOUE**. It was Clement of Alexandria (a headAdoni of the **Didascalia**, the **Catechetical School of Alexandria**, Egypt) who first demonstrated a trans-lettering effort for the pronunciation of the Name using **Greek** letters, **IAOUE. JESU – IESV** The name "Jesus" has only been around for the last few hundred years. IESV is the Christogram used to replace Yahusha in the Roman Catholic's Latin Vulgate. The Anglican Catholic KJV is the Latin Vulgate translated into English. The "J" appeared on the planet less than 500 years ago, so clearly we've been using a mutated form of the original Name for our Savior. The Name "Yahusha" (Yah is our Deliverer, "I am your Deliverer") was given to Yusef in a dream, not the name "Jesus." Those who stubbornly cleave to the recent form "Jesus" and will not listen to reason must ask themselves, what does that mean for all those believers who never used "Jesus" prior to the 16th century? Where's the respect for the Names of the Almighty and His Son, the same respect that we demand for our own personal names? Some feel they can call the Father and His Son by any name of their choosing, yet they feel that **Yahuah** should have their name correct in the *Scroll of Remembrance*, or the Lamb's *Scroll of Life* (whichever scroll it may appear in). Clearly, there is a double-standard toward **Yahuah**'s Name and that of His Son, Yahusha. Men are not endowed with the authority to choose whatever name they prefer to call upon for their salvation, they must submit to Truth, and build on what does not change. We are told in Isaiah 52:6 that **Yahuah**'s people will know His Name. Revelation 3:8 warns us that we are not to deny His Name. Jeremiah 10:25 reveals to us that **Yahuah** will pour out His wrath on those who do not call on His Name. It would be an act of rebellion to ignore these clear instructions; they are not suggestions. ZekarYah 13:9 tells us that those who belong to **Yahuah** will say, "**Yahuah** is the Name of my Alahim." The traditions of our fathers have failed us in this regard. We are told in Revelation 2:13 that we are to hold fast to His Name, but men have not preserved the Truth; it has fallen in the streets. Why did the Pharisees and Priests tell Yahusha's followers not to utter His Name? Because they knew that when Yahusha's Name was being uttered that the Father's Name was being uttered as well because the Father's Name is in His Son, Exodus 23:21.

EXCUSES

Let's examine some of the excuses people use to reject the true Name. Some declare that **Yahuah** has *many* names. No, **Yahuah** has **one** Name and many offices, such as Healer, Shepherd, Redeemer, Father, Husband, Protector, Possessor of Heaven and Earth, etc. Some claim that no matter what name they use, **Yahuah** will know who they mean. This excuse boasts of prideful arrogance, implying that the Creator of Shamayim and Arets will just have to figure it out and deal with the terms **we** choose. It's as if we're naming Him, yet we have no such authority. Others say that the pronunciation of **Yahuah**'s Name has been lost. Do we really believe, even for one moment, that **Yahuah** is going to command us to CALL (*QARA*) upon His Name and then allow the pronunciation to be lost? *Of course not.* All we must do is sound-off the letters; surely we can trust in the most-used word in all of Scripture. The Dead Sea Scrolls have revealed many examples of the original letter form which the Words of Yahuah were written in. Some proclaim that **Yahuah**'s Name is not found in the **Brith Kadasha**. But the reason we don't see **Yahuah**'s Name in the Brith Kadasha is because it has been replaced, and it became *policy* to adopt alternate, popular terms as *substitutions* for it. Titles are not names.

THE FATHER'S NAME

Now let's examine the pronunciation of the Father's name. The 1st century writer called Josephus tells us that the Name consists of *four vowels*. Commonly we see the Name in encyclopedias as **YHWH**. These vowel-letters stand for the Hebrew letters: Yod, Hay, Uau, and Hay. The Yod is the same as our letter **Y**. The Hay is the same as the letter H, and the Uau is often expressed as waw, represented as the *double-u*, but is essentially the sound of oo. The letter Hay appears as the second and fourth letters in the Name. The Assyrians (Ashurim) heard and transcribed the proper transliteration of our Father's Name as Ya-u-a (Yahuah). Having lived with the Israelites who had been taken into captivity by the Assyrians, their transliteration is then creditable. The state of IOWA is said to be based on the Name, handed-down through the native-American tribes. These tribes were remnants of the explorers sent by Solomon to establish *colonies* and mine copper, tin, silver, iron, and gold. Josephus, the first-century historian, recorded in his book Josephus Complete Works, p. 556, that *he had personally seen the golden headpiece worn by the Kohen haGadol.* He described the letters inscribed on the headpiece consisted of *four vowels*. The first two vowel-letters are "Yod Hay" and according to Strong's #H3050 it is pronounced as "Yah." We find an example of this shortened, poetic form of Yahuah's name in Psalms 68:4. The vowels in the original Hebrew were handed down to the Greek, Latin, and English. When we say "Y" we can hear the "i" sound. When we pronounce the "H," we can hear the "a" sound because the "h" is silent, as seen with the name *Sarah*. Vowels are heard without involving the tongue, lips, or teeth, in contrast to consonants which do use these. Now we come to the third vowel-letter Uau, often erroneously rendered Vav/Waw. The UAU is the vowel-letter sound "oo." It is not pronounced as our letter "W," since the Hebrew alef beth does not have a letter to correspond to our W. When the printing press was invented in the mid-1400's, the letter V (Latin sounding as our U) was doubled as a piece of metal type, producing the W. The sixth letter of the Hebrew script should not be thought of as a "double" anything; it's simply a U. So now we have two syllables YaH + U, *YAHU.* The fourth letter of the Name is the vowel-letter Hay. Some believe that the ending of Yahuah's Name has an *-ah* and others *-eh.* The Tribe of *Yahudah* gives us a significant clue. The Name YAHUDAH is spelled: Yod-Hay-Uau-Daleth-Hay. Remove the Daleth which is our D, leaves the four letters, **Yod-Hay-Uau-Hay.**

YAHUDAH – minus the D = YAHUAH

Is it possible to find this truth in the Greek? *Josephus* (Flavius Yusef, born Yusef Ben MatithYahu, 37-101 CE, a Yahudi historian) confirms that our Father's Name consisted of 4 vowels, with the UAU having the "oo" sound which agrees with the Assyrian pronunciation *Ya-u-a*, and is pronounced **YAHUAH.** Strong's #H3068 (6823 entries) renders Yahuah's name as *Yehovah*, which is inaccurate. Checking H3050 we find that His shortened, poetic name, **YaH**, refers us right back to H3068, which which they rendered as "Yeh..." **Yah** is correct; **Yeh** is an alteration. The **Yeh** spelling is the result of the **Masoretes**, who used alternative vowels from another word, **adonai**, in order to keep the Name of Yahuah concealed from the masses, thus *perpetuating the ban of pronouncing the Name aloud.* The vowel-pointing by the Masoretes cannot be trusted because of their intention to hide the Name of our Father, **Yahuah**. The vowels they used were intended to direct the reader to say **ADONAI** instead of what was written - it was to cue the reader to not pronounce the Name! In the Name Yahusha, Ya/Yah was changed to Ye/Yeh which hides the connection with the Name of the Father, Exodus 23:21. Another confirmation is found in The **Stromata**, v. 6, by Clement of Alexandria:

"**...the mystic name of the four letters which was affixed to those alone to whom the *adytum was accessible, is called 'IAOUE' which is interpreted, Who is and shall** be." *[An **adytum** was the innermost sanctuary of an ancient Greek temple]*

How then does "ahayah/I Am" fit into our understanding of Father's Name? At Exodus 3:14 we read, "... ahayah Asher ahayah: and He said, 'This shall you say to the children of Yisharal, ahayah has sent me to you.'" **Ahayah Asher ahayah** means "I will be Who I will be." When Father spoke "ahayah Asher ahayah," He was speaking of Himself in the first person because only He could say "I will be," whereas when He reveals to His people that His Name is Yahuah, He is speaking in the third person. **Yahuah** is the Name we are to know, declare, and worship through the Name Yahusha, "I am your Deliverer." He identifies Himself exclusively by this one Name. Yahusha clearly tells us in John 17:26 that He had declared His Father's Name to the people and since we are Yahusha's body, we are to do the same, Kolossians 1:18. How foolish to think that the Head, Yahusha would call His Father **Yahuah** (Yahuah), but His body (us) would call our Father, LORD, God or Jehovah makes no sense, does it? Again, how can Yahuah's Name be "Jehovah" and the Son's Name be "Jesus" since there is no "J" in Hebrew? The apostle "John" is really "Yahukanon." At John 5:43 Yahusha tells us that He came in His Father's Name. He came in the authority of Yahuah, and carries this Name in His own. Jeremiah (YirmeYahu) 23:25-27 tells us that "lies" have caused **Yahuah**'s people to forget His Name for Bel, "**LORD**." Many faulty interpretations have been propagated through the leadership in both Judaism and Christianity. Not only have Judaism and Christianity replaced the Names of the Father and His Son, but they've even changed the original palaeo-Hebrew names of the prophets in order to conceal **Yahuah**'s Name because this Name is embedded in the original names of several prophets. An example of this is found in the name of the prophet known as "Jeremiah." In palaeo-Hebrew, his name contains the shortened, poetic form of Father's Name, "Yah" and should have been transliterated as *YirmeYahu* (see any concordance). Notice that it ends with "Yah." The word "Isaiah" should be rendered *YashaYahu*. Notice the ending "**iah**" in these two names. The prophets would not recognize their own names as they are transliterated in our modern-day English Scriptures.

THE SON'S NAME

Hebrews 13:8 tells us Yahusha is the same yesterday, today and forever. So do we really believe that He has changed His Name from Hebrew to a Greco/Roman/English name? Of course not! And we learn from Philippians 2:9 that His Name is above every name. Would that include His Father's Name? No, it wouldn't and here's why: again, Exodus 23:21 tells us that the Father's Name is in His Son. The Father and His Son share the shortened, poetic name "Yah." Acts 4:12 tells us there is no other name by which we can be delivered. This Hebrew Name is:

Yod-Hay-Uau-Shin-Ayin: Yahusha

This script is read right-to-left. Notice that the first three vowel-letters are exactly the same as the Father's name "**Yahu**." Next we have the letter "shin" which is "sh" and finally the "Ayin" which is essentially silent but is represented by a rough breathing sound in the back of the throat. Hebrew is read/written right-to-left. The Greco/Roman/English name ***Jesus*** would have been unknown to Yahusha. *Jesus* has no meaning in Hebrew, whereas Yahusha means "Yah, He is salvation" or literally **"I am your Deliverer."** The one who hung on the stake/tree for us was named Yahusha, not someone named Jesus. Why is it that most believers readily accept the free gift of His finished work at Golgatha, but refuse to acknowledge Him by His Hebrew Name which was given to Him by His Father, **Yahuah**? We must teach people to call on His Hebrew Name for salvation but regretfully that has not been the case in the Kirche (Church). If we take a closer look at the Paleo Hebrew name for Joshua, we find that it is the clearest example of how our Savior's Name is spelled and pronounced. Strong's #H3091 spells Joshua's name in Paleo Hebrew as "Yod Hay Uau Shin Ayin," this is exactly how we spell Yahusha's Name as well. Some add another UAU after the SHIN, and that is perfectly acceptable. *[compare YARUSHA at 2Mal. 15:33]* Here's something very enlightening: if we look up the name "Jesus" in Strong's #G2424 it is sounded out as "ee-ay-sooce," but refers us right back to Joshua in Strong's #H3091 "Yeho shua." For further proof, we go to Acts 7:45, where we find the name Joshua in our English Scriptures, but what's amazing is that it is the exact same number in Strong's #G2424 which is used for the name "Jesus." Names are always transliterated from the source language to the target language by their sounds. Names have meanings, but it is not proper to translate them. Names should be **transliterated** by the **sound** of each letter no matter what the alphabets used may be, just as our own name in English will always sound the same no matter what foreign alphabet it may be converted into. What do we do with the alternative spellings such as *Y'shua, Yeshua or Yahshua*? Some claim that Y'shua or Yeshua is the shortened, *Aramaic* form for His Name. Others declare that Yeshua is a form of **Yeshu**, an unscriptural **acronym** for Yahusha's Name standing for **Ye**mak **Sh**mo **U'**Zikro, meaning *may his name be blotted out.* So we can see why this would be a name that the enemy would like us to use because every time we speak Yeshua, we are in essence declaring that His Name be blotted out. The form Yah_shua leaves out the "uau" which is the vowel-letter sound "oo." 2 Timothy 2:15 tells us we are to "rightly divide the word of truth." What was hidden or whispered in secret is now being shouted from the rooftops. We learn at Acts 9:15 that Shaul/Paul was to bear Yahusha's Name before the Guyim. It is impossible for Shaul to have declared the Greco/Roman/English name "Jesus." Paul declared the Name of **Yahusha**; and as His body, so must we. Shaul was sent to arrest and kill those who **called** upon the true Name. Following his own conversion to the

Truth of the Name (by Yahusha Himself), he used it boldly and was stoned several times for it. They wouldn't have stoned him if he had used the **name of error** we have inherited. **We must make a decision. How long do we waver between two opinions? This controversy was settled at Mt. Karmel by AliYahu, and the priests of Bel and Asherah were all killed. The Name is being brought forth for the final battle.** If Yahuah is Alahim, then serve Him; if Bel (Lord) is Alahim, serve him. Do we call our Creator and His Son by unreal names and common titles which Rabbinical Judaism and Christianity have traditionally deceived us with, or do we return to the ancient, palaeo-Hebrew written by the finger of **Yahuah**/YaHUaH? If Scripture is the final authority in our lives, then the answer is very clear. **Yahuah** and **Yahusha** are the truest sound we can make from the letters we have received in Hebrew. Yahusha revealed that He is Al Shaddai at Revelation 1:8, explaining the mysterious use of the identity marker, **ALEF-TAU** throughout the TaNaK. Yahuah is "ONE", and He became flesh and dwelled among us in the form of a man. The Name is the *Key of knowledge* which has been withheld from us, and it will unlock the revealed Word to any who accept it, giving understanding and wisdom to the simple. Yahusha has revealed His identity through the ALEF-TAU revelation. The very idea there is a "key" validates that there is something to be unlocked. The Besorah is the *message* of Yahusha, and we who know it must carry it to warn the Guyim. He said He would be with us, and only ONE Being is capable of existing in more than one place at the same time. Now you know Who the Father is, and Who the Son is. This book is His warning message to all mankind, to teach us how **to love Him**, and **love one another**. Truly, He will help us do that, and fulfill His purpose for us.

THE MESSAGE OF LOVE

The Besorah is the *message* given to prophets selected by the Creator Being, YAHUAH (**Yahuah**) to all mankind. This *message* is both a record of specific events, and a revelation of the plan of redemption and restoration. The original parents of all mankind were perfect, created to live in **Eden** (bliss, delight), and they were deathless. They were deceived by a fallen creature that brought doubt into believing the Word of **Yahuah**, and so they failed a simple test: believing what He had spoken. Through this error, *death entered the world. Life* and *death* are on display throughout the entire message, and **Yahuah** calls out to all men to *choose life*, by believing in His Word, and proving they believe it by *obeying* Him. This choice is made by believing His Word, the *message* (Hebrew, *besorah*), and living by it, according to the Covenant given to a chosen people He selected (Yisharal / Israel).

BYNV – HOW IT IS DIFFERENT
Whatever translation you may own, check Mt. 26:17 and Mark 14:12. If it reads "On the first day of unleavened bread" they used the **KJV*** for their framework. You can't look for a place to observe Passover when it's already happened. The 1st day of Matsah is the 15th day of the 1st moon, Passover lambs were killed on the 14th. There is no word "day" used here, and the word "protos" should read "**prior to** Unleavened Bread."
*The KJV is **Angican Catholic**, and the translators used the **Latin Vulgate** to produce an English version. The Latin Vulgate used a Christogram for the Name of Yahusha: IESV. **IESV** is shown in the first edition of the KJV. More importantly, the *personal Name* of the Creator is deleted from most English translations, substituted with the word "LORD" and in some cases the word "GOD." In this BYNV, the Name is restored in the places it occurs in the inspired text, and other names are also more accurately transliterated, eliminating the distortions caused by the Greek and Latin alphabets. Greek terms such as "Genesis" and "Exodus" are

accompanied by the authentic Hebrew terms. Hebrew is the *lashon qodesh*, or *qodesh tongue*, so restoring the names without distortion enables the reader to experience the richness, purity, and authenticity that flows from the unfiltered, inspired words in the Creator's Mind. The *key of knowledge* is the personal Name of the Creator, and using it unlocks the message that would otherwise remain sealed from our comprehension. A name uniquely identifies who is being spoken of. The first known *translation* of Yahuah's Word was made from Hebrew into the Greek language between 285-246 BCE for a Ptolemaic king at Alexandria, Egypt. That translation is often referred to as the Septuagint, or the Latin designation, LXX. **Septuagint** is Latin for *seventy*. It was assumed that 70 scribes were used to translate the **Turah** (5 books of Mushah) into Greek. When they did so, they left the Name of the Highest One Alahim unmolested, **as this translation also does.** The digital version of the BYNV phonetically expresses the Hebrew letter sounds, but the printed version of this BYNV is one of the few times since the LXX a translation has been made that leaves the original Name as it appeared in the Hebrew. Lies inherited from our fathers are being overcome with Truth.

THE SCRIPT: AN HISTORICAL CONTEXT

The original autograph of the Creator is best shown using the ancient, primary letters He used to write His Name with His finger at Sinai, and that form looks like this: **Yahuah**. The world has called this letter style *Phoenician*, not realizing that the label, *Phoenician*, was bestowed upon the Israelites by the Greek writers, a word meaning "date palm" in Greek. The Latin *punic wars* is a reference to the wars against the Hebrews. The word *Phoenix* (Latin *poenus*) means the same thing, and the later Roman empire converted this word into *Punic* when they were battling their Israelite enemies at Carthage. The **Yisharalites** have been called many things by the land empires over the ages, such as *Carthaginians*,

Parthians, or *Scythians;* but as *Phoenicians* they are best known as a *sea people*. The Yisharalites dwelled in the land given to them by Yahuah, however they were more of a "sea empire" than a *land empire*. When you see other sources describing the script seen in this book as **Phoenician**, you can understand how this term applies to the *Yisharalite* empire as it was known to the Greeks. The house of Yisharal made alliances with Tyre and Sidon, causing the northern 10 tribes to fall into Bel worship, and for this they were scattered into the Guyim by the Assyrian empire (circa 722 BCE). Scholars refer to the "Israelites," and call the land "Canaan" before Yahuah drove out its inhabitants. A small part of the coastline was known as "Filistia," which the Romans later adopted as their reference, *Palestine*. Scholars commonly believe that the tribes of Yisharal adopted their alef-beth (alphabet) from the residents of Canaan (Byblos, Tyre, Sidon), but the reverse is the case. The Semitic language and 22-lettered alef-beth was common to all descendants of Shem. The name of Shem gives us the term **Shemite**, losing the "sh" sound by passing through the Greek language, and becoming "Semite." **WHAT IS THE WARNING MESSAGE? Repent, for the reign of Yahuah draws near!** He said, "**Love Me, and guard My Commandments.**" The Word, Light, Wisdom, Living Water, and His Covenant are all one and the same thing: the **Turah of Yahuah**. The Turah teaches us <u>how</u> to love. **Without love, Creation has no purpose.**

The Mashiak, Yahusha of Natsarith, told an elder of Yisharal (Israel):

"If you do not believe when I spoke to you about earthly things, how are you going to believe when I speak to you about the heavenly things? And no one has gone up into the heavens except He who came down from the heavens – the Son of Adam. And as Mushah lifted up the serpent in the wilderness, even so must the Son of Adam be lifted up, so that whosoever believes in Him should not perish

but possess everlasting life. For Alahim so loved the world that He gave His only procreated Son, so that everyone who believes in Him should not perish but possess everlasting life. For Alahim did not send His Son into the world to judge the world, but that the world through Him might be saved. He who believes in Him is not judged, but he who does not believe is judged already, because he has not believed in the Name of the only procreated Son of Alahim. And this is the judgment, that the light has come into the world, and men loved the darkness rather than the light, for their works were evil. For everyone who practices evil hates the light and does not come to the light, lest his works should be exposed. But the one doing the truth comes to the light, so that his works are clearly seen, that they have been wrought in **Alahim."** -Yahukanon 3

"And He Himself is an atoning slaughter for our sins, and not for ours only but also for all the world. And by this we know that we know Him, if we guard His commands. The one who says, 'I know Him,' and does not guard His commands, is a liar, and the truth is not in him. But whoever guards His Word, truly the love of Alahim has been perfected in him. By this we know that we are in Him: The one who says he stays in Him ought himself also to walk, even as He walked. Beloved, I write no recent command to you, but an original command which you have had from the beginning. The original command is the Word which you heard from the beginning."
1 Yahukanon (**Turah** is the original command)

DAVID - OR DAUD?
The contemporary English spelling of this great ruler is **David**, and often people say "**da-VEED**" to adopt a more modern Hebrew posture. Modern Hebrew is different in some aspects from the authentic 22 letters. The 6th letter, **UAU**, has morphed into WAW. The influences of foreign languages have

caused this letter to become a VAV, but it is simply a U. This name is spelled with 3 letters, DALETH-UAU-DALETH, or literally DUD in our English. It will be rendered Daud, to suggest the pronunciation as **da-OOD**.

Replacement Theology
The Christian concept known as replacement theology (or Supersessionism) proposes their idea of a "New Covenant" supersedes the Abrahimic, Moshaic, and Daudic Covenants, and the moral teachings that define sin are altered. The people of Yisharal are now considered to be replaced by Christian believers, who inherit all the promises made to Yisharal. They usurp the title "Yisharal" under the label "Spiritual Israel." Engrafting to Yisharal through the **everlasting Covenant** is regarded as heresy. YirmeYahu (Jer.) 31 quickly reveals the error of this thinking. The foundation of our path must be the Word of Yahuah, and yet traditions grew up like weeds that severed all the "Hebrew roots." The pagan priesthood at Rome slowly transformed into the chimera (mixed beasts) we see, but do not perceive. A contemporary word for this "beast" would be monster, or a monstrosity. Constantine I altered the 10 Commandments by honoring Apollo/Mithras instead of Yahuah, the Creator. His edict in 321 made "Sunday" the weekly day of rest.
The **sign** of the everlasting Covenant, Shabath, was considered "Judaizing," and anyone resting on the proper day known as "the **Sabbath**" at the Council of Laodicea (circa 365 CE) was labelled a heretic. Obeying the Shabath Command marked a person as a heretic (anathema, worthy of death). The 4th Commandment, the **sign** between Yahuah and His people forever, was directly attacked (defiled). Rome was the funding and enforcement, and Alexandria was the doctrinal center of the replacement theology. The **Didascalia**, or Catechetical School at Alexandria, severed all Hebrew roots through men who were harshly anti-Semitic: the **church**

fathers. Their allegorical interpretations made it appear that Christians replaced Yisharal, and inherited all the promises, without any obligation to obey Turah. **Turah of Yahuah**, also know as the **Turah of Mushah** The Turah was given to Mushah to teach the congregation, and the world not yet born, and is mentioned at Acts 15 in the decisions reached by the Ruach ha Qodesh, Yaqub (Yahusha's brother), Kefa, and the chief supports of the Natsarim. The Guyim engrafting into the Covenant were to begin with 4 main points, and continue to learn the **Turah of Yahuah**, since their parents had been idolaters. Notice this idea is expressed at Acts 15. The Turah (Mushah) is read in the congregations, every Shabath:
Act 15:21 **"For from ancient generations Mushah has, in every city, those proclaiming him – being read** in the congregations every **Shabath."** **Why the Earth Will Be Burned** MatithYahu 24 matches the message of YashaYahu (Isaiah) 24, but notice this passage in particular:
YashaYahu 24:5, 6: "For the arets has been defiled under its inhabitants, because they have transgressed the Turoth, changed the law, broken the **everlasting Covenant**. Therefore a curse shall consume the earth, and those who dwell in it be punished. Therefore the inhabitants of the earth shall be **burned**, and few men shall be left."
This is one of many warnings, such as Malaki 4:4-6, and Yual chapters 2 & 3.
This is the reason the earth will be burned in the day of judgment. The sacraments have been used to ensnare hearts through empty deceit, and are the traditions of men, Kolossians 2. **The Renewed Covenant** The "renewed Covenant" is "Mashiak in you," the promised Paraklita (Helper) that comes into our heart to inscribe His Turah on our hearts. Yahusha circumcises the hearts and minds of His followers, enabling them to receive His Mind, and to see their Teacher's point-of-view. The Natsarim, the original followers of Yahusha, realized He had come into them as He had promised. **The Old Covenant** was written on a **scroll** and

placed **beside** the ark (see Dt. 31:26, Hebrews 8). It relied on animal blood to atone for unintentional sins. Animal blood could never redeem permanently, so it and the priesthood that implemented it has grown old and disappeared, replaced by a renewed Covenant that redeems completely. **The Renewed Covenant** is through Yahusha's blood, which ended the hand-written procedures on the scroll beside the ark. The confusion is dispelled when one understands the Ten Commandments are not the "old" covenant. The Commandments were written by the finger of Yahuah on **stone tablets** and placed **inside** the ark, not beside it. Yahusha writes a love for the Torah on our hearts of flesh, which is our inward circumcision by Mashiak, sealing us with His Name at our immersion for the day of our redemption. He now lives in His redeemed, enabling them through His power to live in steadfast obedience. **The First-fruits** Those obeying the Turah of Yahuah and holding to the Testimony of Yahusha are the first-fruits, and the target of the dragon. We identify a tree by its fruit, so if we work out who has been the doctrinal source of the persecuting, we will find the servant of the dragon: the malicious prophet. *See also YashaYahu/Isa 13:9, 13:11, 26:21, 66:24, Mikah 5:15, ZefanYah 1:2-18, YirmeYahu/Jer 23:36.

      BYNV (Besorah of Yahusha Natsarim Version).

Taking Scripture At Its Word Isn't Popular

A day is set, infinitely scarier than Halloween. The nations may rage, but Yahusha's culture will be the only one left standing when He returns, and the pure lip will be restored. Greek will be remembered no more. The Torah will go forth from Yerushalom, and His Name will be one. Yahusha is obsessed over His bride, and those who do not wish Him to reign over them will be brought before Him for their execution, and this is why we are warning those who will listen to the Truth. YashaYahu (Isaiah) 24, Malaki 4:1-6, and Yual (Joel) 2 are prophecies not to be treated lightly. Reapers are waiting to harvest the Earth, and Natsarim are here sounding the warning. www.fossilizedcustoms.com/reapers.html

What we say and do is the result of how we were taught.

If you want to unlearn the error, please keep reading.

This is what you are not hearing in the steeples, and the Truth is going to make you sad at first, because it is so simple.
"Come out of her, My people!" will make sense.

The teachers who have been lying to the crowds will become enraged. *Phonology* is the study of the *sound* of a language.

In the case of the inspired Word of Yahuah, there has been a long-standing resistance to uttering the Name by translators.

In the 8th century, a sophisticated method using vowel marks was developed, and it has been promoted successfully for many centuries and is the official delusion now. It has been the primary lock keeping everyone from calling on the Name.

We have the Key, and we're the guardians of the Name.

We are the Natsarim, the first followers of Yahusha.

Here in the last days, Yahusha is awakening His bride, those having stored up the extra oil of His Name. The conspiracy to conceal His Name is being shouted from the rooftops.

This is the apostasy (***falling-away***) that must come first.
(2 Thess. 2:3)

Are you feeling the urges from Yahusha to fall away from men's teachings?

One of the problems of getting to the Truth has always been a teaching authority stepping in to make it seem the "lay person" doesn't have the capacity, training, or permission granted to them to teach. This was how they treated Yahusha, because He released so much Truth He became a threat to the fragile egos of those controlling teachings. Yahusha is our Teacher, not traditions invented by men. The Name is the Key of knowledge, the Rock rejected by the builders. (Ps. 118:26)

In 2008, a **papal bull** issued by the pope gave orders to the bishops (elders in the RCC) to prohibit the use of the true Name as expressed in the Tetragrammaton (4 letters) for the Name of our Creator. They were ordered to substitute it with other traditional terms, such as Dominus or LORD. On the road to Damascus, Shaul was sent to arrest anyone, even in foreign cities, who was found pronouncing the Name. He was to shackle them and carry them back to the Sanhedrin, where they were to be destroyed by stoning. On his way, Shaul met the resurrected Yahusha, Who spoke to him in the Hebrew language. This was Shaul's first encounter with Yahusha, and it changed him so much that he became one of us.

This Is The Way, Walk In It
Obedience is better than burnt offerings. Most people live and die without hearing the Truth. Hebrews 8:13 is telling us the animal blood and old priesthood is now obsolete, not the Ten Commandments. The old covenant was hand-written on a scroll placed BESIDE the ark (Dt. 31:26).
Christians are taught to disobey by their pastors, not understanding the "old" covenant was the old priesthood and animal blood offered as atonement.
The Ten Commandments are cast aside, but they will be the standard used on the day of judgment.
The Ten Commandments were INSIDE the ark, written in stone by Yahuah's finger, now written on our hearts by the Spirit of Yahusha. See Yekezqal (Ez.) 36:26
Billions are fed WORMWOOD, altered teachings. The whole Earth will be burned for breaking the "everlasting Covenant." Read about it at YashaYahu (Is.) 24. Even if the heavens and Earth pass away, the Ten Commandments will never pass away. They teach us what LOVE looks like.
This book (LOVE) emphasizes obedience to the everlasting Covenant in order for many to be restored to favor with Yahusha. His blood takes our sins away, not the Commandments telling us what sin is (1 Yn. 3:4).

The renewed Covenant is sealed in the blood offered by Yahusha, and redeems completely. Animal blood and the old priesthood could never do this. Read all of YirmeYahu 31:33; it predicts the Torah **written on our hearts**, and how permanent and secure the everlasting Covenant INSIDE the ark really is, now that He has given us a love for it.

To believe we can ignore His Commandments, and yet say we have repented of sin, is confusion. Most have only repented of the Commandments, not sin, and their teachers are responsible. Has anyone yet read Malaki 4:1-6?

"And this is the love, that we walk according to His commands. This is the command, that as you have heard from the beginning, you should walk in it. Because many who are leading astray went out into the world who do not admit Yahusha Mashiak as coming in the flesh. This one is he who is leading astray and the anti-Mashiak.* See to yourselves, that we do not lose what we worked for, but that we might receive a complete reward. Everyone who is transgressing and not staying in the teaching of Mashiak does not possess Yahuah. The one who stays in the teaching of Mashiak possesses both the Father and the Son. If anyone comes to you and does not bring this teaching, do not receive him into your house nor greet him, for he who greets him shares in his wicked works." (2 Yn. 1:6-11)

*[This was a Gnostic teaching, since those who denied Yahusha coming in flesh thought everything *physical* was evil. Some were being taught Yahusha was only an ephemera, or manifestation]

"For this is the love for Yahuah, that we guard His commands, and His commands are not difficult, because everyone having been begotten of Yahuah overcomes the world." (1 Yn. 5:3-4)

"Everyone doing sin also does lawlessness, and sin is lawlessness." (1 Yn. 3:4)

Yahuah Is An Alahim Of Lawfulness

This means that He expects obedience, not for us to ignore His Commandments because we think they have been "done away" somehow. The old process for atonement is what has been "done away" with.

"1000 flee at the rebuke of one; at the rebuke of 5 you shall flee until you are left as a pole on top of a mountain and as a sign on a hill. And therefore Yahuah shall wait, to show you favor. And therefore He shall be exalted, to have compassion on you.
For Yahuah is an Alahim of lawfulness.
Blessed are all those who wait for Him.
For the people shall dwell in Tsiun at Yerushalim, you shall weep no more. He shall show much favor to you at the sound of your cry; when He hears, He shall answer you. Though Yahuah gave you bread of adversity and water of affliction, your Teacher shall no longer be hidden. But your eyes shall see your Teacher, and your ears hear a word behind you, saying, "This is the Way, walk in it," whenever you turn to the right, or whenever you turn to the left." YashaYahu (Isaiah) 30:17-21

The Spirit of Error

"Beloved ones, do not believe every Ruach, but prove the ruachs, whether they are of Yahuah, because many false prophets have gone out into the world. By this you know the Ruach of Yahuah: Every Ruach that admites that Yahusha Mashiak has come in the flesh is of Yahuah, and every ruach that does not admit that Yahusha Mashiak has come in the flesh is not of Yahuah. And this is the ruach of the anti-Mashiak which you heard is coming, and now is already in the world. You are of Yahuah, little children, and have overcome them, because He who is in you is greater than he who is in the world. They are of the world, therefore they speak as of the world, and the world hears them. We are of Yahuah – the one knowing Yahuah hears us. He who is not of Yahuah does

not hear us. By this we know the Ruach of the Truth and the ruach of the delusion. Beloved ones, let us love one another, because love is of Yahuah, and everyone who loves has been born of Yahuah, and knows Yahuah. The one who does not love does not know Yahuah, for Yahuah is love. By this the love of Yahuah was manifested in us, that Yahuah has sent His only begotten Son into the world, in order that we might live through Him. In this is love, not that we loved Yahuah, but that He loved us and sent His Son to be an atoning offering for our sins. 11Beloved ones, if Yahuah so loved us, we also ought to love one another. No one has seen Yahuah at any time.
If we love one another, Yahuah does stay in us, and His love has been perfected in us. By this we know that we stay in Him, and He in us, because He has given us of His Ruach."
1 Yahukanon 4:1-13

If one of the first Natsarim were to somehow be taken from their time and place and brought forward to see what people think and do now, they would not recognize, or believe what they would see.

Once sound teachings are received from Scripture, deception is less likely. We cannot approach Scripture with pre-conceived ideas and then hunt-down texts to validate what we already believe. Let Scripture teach, and allow the context to inform the meaning. The Latin Vulgate (late 4th century) twisted Malaki 4:2 into "the **Sun** of righteousness," but the context and meaning of the word SHAMASH should have been rendered **Servant**, not the **Sun**.
If a Seminary professor from any Christian institution were to stand next to one of first Natsarim and compare notes, one could honestly say their walk is found in the Scripture of Truth, but the other would find no evidence of their walk in Scripture. The Christian would be unable to do anything the other practiced due to men's traditions completely overwhelming

their world view. Obeying Commandments is legalistic to the Christian walk, yet the Natsarim establish the idea.

When you come to learn that He is Yahuah, our Redeemer, you will become one of the Natsarim. He said, "Ani ha Gafen (I am the Vine), atah ha Natsarim (you are the branches)." Baruk haba bashem Yahuah.

How are Natsarim different from Christians?
Both claim to follow the same Person, yet in practice differ in every way.

Always use Scripture (the Word) to correct, rebuke, teach, and train in righteousness. Would anyone reading these words believe that satan now wants us to obey the Word, teach all nations to walk as Yahusha walked, and call on His Name? The whole world has been deceived, and has gone mad with trees, wreaths, rabbits, eggs, birthday cakes and wishes, following the guru in their midst who teaches them to eat pigs and meet at pillars on the Day of the Sun.
They have set aside the appointments, and replaced them with their own desires.
Read the global curse at Malaki 4:1-6. The elements will melt with fervent heat in the wrath of His displeasure.

The 7th month begins with the Day of the Shout (ram's horn is heard). Let's repent of all the Hindu/Nimrodland activities, purging the leaven of men's traditions. All who call on the Name of Yahuah will be delivered, and He has become our Deliverer: YAHUSHA. Stay away from the towers and domes, stop teaching children about Santa (Christmas), Halloween (necromancy), and eggs/bunnies and fertility customs (Easter is the name of the earth mother). Yahusha is near.
Stop praying for Yahuah to do your will; ask Him to tell you what He wants you to do so others will come to know Him.

Why Does The Universe Exist In One Sentence?
The universe exists to be an environment for the companions Yahuah created: beings that love one another.

Great Commission Unpacked
Love Yahuah, love nearby beings (neighbors).
Endtime Watchmen, follow youtube link to watch:
https://youtu.be/EBrqFYhIDg0

Origin Of The Word BIBLE
Many people hear the Truth, and are not affected by it at all. Byblus / Byblos was the location of the temple of BYBLIA, and the primary export trade was parchment made from flax. The word Bible was adopted by the Greek culture and referred to parchments, and is now used to refer to Yahuah's Writings of Truth (Kethab Amath, Danial 10:21, yet it is only on the cover due to tradition. Should we refer to Yahuah's Word by the town named after a female fertility deity, or use the term He used for His Writings?
The ultimate source of Truth is in the Word of Yahuah, and one could read His Word and gain wisdom, and meet the Writer Himself if one diligently seeks Him. Reading His Word renews our minds, and we learn what pleases Him.
Disobedience is never going to please Yahusha.
What does Yahuah's Word call itself?
Kethab Amath (Scripture of Truth) is the Eberith (Hebrew) used at Danial 10:21 that we should call Yahuah's Word.

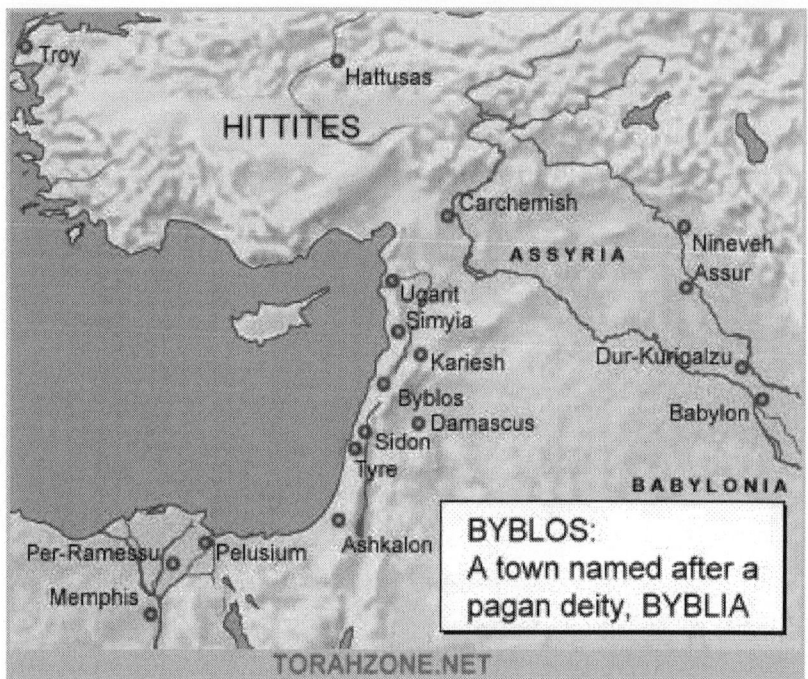

It is impossible to repent while continuing to sin.

We are ambassadors sent to free the prisoners imprisoned by the stronghold of faulty thinking. Christian doctrines promote sin. They have received a spirit of error.
To be legal is heretical in their minds, and accomplishes the will of Nimrod, Izebel, Antiochus Epiphanes, and Constantine. In Scripture, there is no such thing as a way of living called CHRISTIANITY.
People need to see things from Yahuah's perspective, not man's traditions. Those who worship Yahuah do so in Truth, not through religion. Truth is reality, tradition is religion.

GOD is a concept from the land of Nimrod, the mighty one behind all the pagan Sun deities and part of the Babel effect. It infected the whole world by the Silk Road out of India around 200 BCE when it brought Gnostic ideas into the Middle East. Confusion exploded. Yahuah exists, and every knee will bow to Him, in Shamayim and arets very soon. Mystagogues draw your attention away from the Truth, but the

Natsarim possess the greatest treasure of all: the presence of our Creator in their jars of clay. Google Yahusha, and please wake up.

Day Of The Shout
1Thess. 4:16:
"For Yahuah Himself will descend from shamayim with a shout, with the voice of a Chief Messenger, and with the shofar of Alahim, and the dead in Mashiak will rise first."
The 7th month begins with the Day of the Shout (ram's horn is heard).
Let's repent of all the Hindu/Nimrodland activities, purging the leaven of men's traditions. All who call on the Name of Yahuah will be delivered, and He has become our Deliverer: YAHUSHA

Yahusha Is Not Our Shabath
It is impossible to please Yahuah by being disobedient and hating His instructions (Ps. 50:17). Until we accept Yahuah's Covenant, He will not allow us to receive His Name. Yahusha has one Name, and YashaYahu 42:8 confirms that His Name is Yahuah, and YashaYahu 43:11 confirms there is no other Deliverer besides Him. The false teaching (stronghold) that JESUS is the name we are to call on for our deliverance is very dangerous, and goes against the teachings of Yual (Joel isn't his name either) chapters 2 & 3. Yahusha's Natsarim are not to condemn people, only teachings that are misleading the untaught who are stumbling in darkness. Natsarim are patient, kind, gentle, joyful, peaceful, loving, and show more of Yahusha's fruits, and they hear only their Shepherd's voice in one another. Discern the tree by the fruit you see being produced. Use Scripture to correct and train. The Ten Commandments teach love, and are easy to obey. Yahusha is the Master of Shabath (Mt. 12:8 and two other verses), so Constantine and the council of Laodicea can never change that. Mt. 24:20 is a reference to Shabath during the last days,

and Yahusha told us to pray our flight would not be in winter or on the Shabath. Yahusha is not our Shabath, He is the Master of Shabath. This means He is the Creator Who instituted the 7th day we are to rest, even as He rested. Hebrews 4 refers directly to this fact. YirmeYahu 10:25 asks Yahuah to pour out His wrath on the guyim who do not call on His Name. In the seventh month one of these years, His wrath will pour out.
www.fossilizedcustoms.com/transliteration.html

The 7 appointed times were replaced with 7 sacraments.

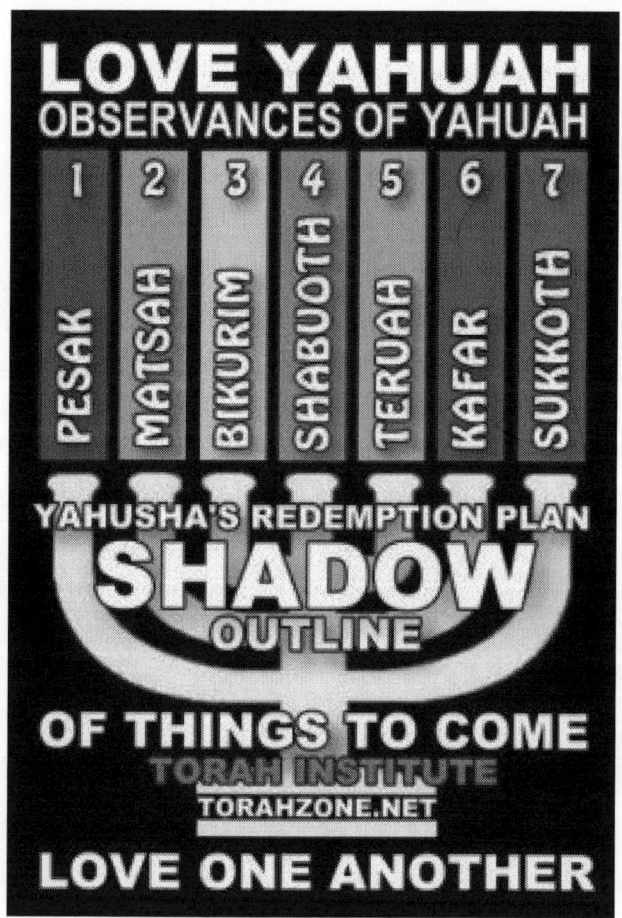

Sacraments can't help you please Yahusha

Page one of a 4-page tract is shown here. You can find the whole tract as a free download at torahzone.net

CHRISTIANS ARE IN TROUBLE

PASTORS ARE LEARNING ABOUT THEIR TRADITIONS

"Christians Are In Trouble" - says resigned pastor . . . **Christian pastors know there is something wrong with their traditions.** They perceive a circular pattern in their festivals, then discover the outward crust is only masking their origins: the worship of the host of heaven.

THERE IS A GLOBAL CURSE GIVEN AT MALAKI 4 YOU NEED TO READ

Christmas, New Year, Valentines, Easter, Mother & Father Days, and Halloween are celebrated world-wide, and merchants promote each of these fertility festivals many weeks ahead to exploit the sleeping hypnotized crowds. Their pastors sit and watch, never blowing the shofar to warn anyone. Their doctrines are built on sand, and do not follow the Scripture of Truth, so their witness is without a firm foundation. **If you begin to do what is written in the Word, they ask you to depart from their assembly.**

Christian pastors are resigning all around the world to serve Yahusha, not their denomination's orders. One pastor came out saying Christians are in trouble: "We want to come into more understanding about certain doctrines and desire to be baptized in the Name of our Savior Yahusha to the [esteem] of Yahuah. Myself in Christianity was a preacher with General licence . . . . . Me and my wife resigned from religion on 11 December 2018. 14th December we came shockingly unto the un-

WHO ARE CHRISTIANS?
Without knowing it, Christians are followers of a Greco-Roman culture of names, terms, and festivals, all adopted intact from

pagan sources, yet adapted and mixed carefully with ideas and people from the Hebrew Scriptures.

Mixing together the practices and beliefs of an ingenous population is missionary adaptation, called **syncretism**. These heresies from the *reign of Babel* began to take root through the teachings of Simon Magus, and through councils eventually became the basis for the teaching authority known as the Catechetical School at Alexandria (C.S.A.) under its first headmaster, Pantaenus in 190 CE.

This institution set up the frameword that eventually came to dominate the beliefs and practices of the entire western world. The **Great Schism** of 1054 CE produced the rift between the western empire Roman Catholic Magisterium at Rome and Eastern Orthodox Catholicism. Later the Reformation in the 16th century further fragmented the movement when the nobility rejected the papal authority at Rome; but much error remained from the adherence to the early church fathers and their writings. These church fathers persecuted and despised the first followers of Yahusha, the Natsarim, and wrote about us. They considered us heretics because we obey the Torah. Every detail of **Scriptural observance** was omitted by the church fathers, and replaced with new observances.

With skillfully-crafted reasoning over many centuries, the formerly pagan observances were camouflaged or wrapped in new meanings, believing to be cleansed of their filth, and now loved and cherished by their LORD. Yahusha would never teach the things they do.

Examples:

Sacraments - Yahuah never commanded them, hinted at them indirectly, or mentioned any such thing. They add to the Torah, against Dt. 12.

Sun-day - the Day of the Sun. Many other even stranger festivals were invented, all being adaptations from former Sun worship.

SUNDAY ORIGINS – SUN WORSHIP'S SPECIAL DAY

(Most all the headmasters at Alexandria were former worshippers of the Sun. The cult of Sun worshippers at Alexandria, Egypt worshipped Osiris and called themselves Christians in the 2nd century BCE by bowing to cross-shapes, used by Sun worshipping pagans world-wide)

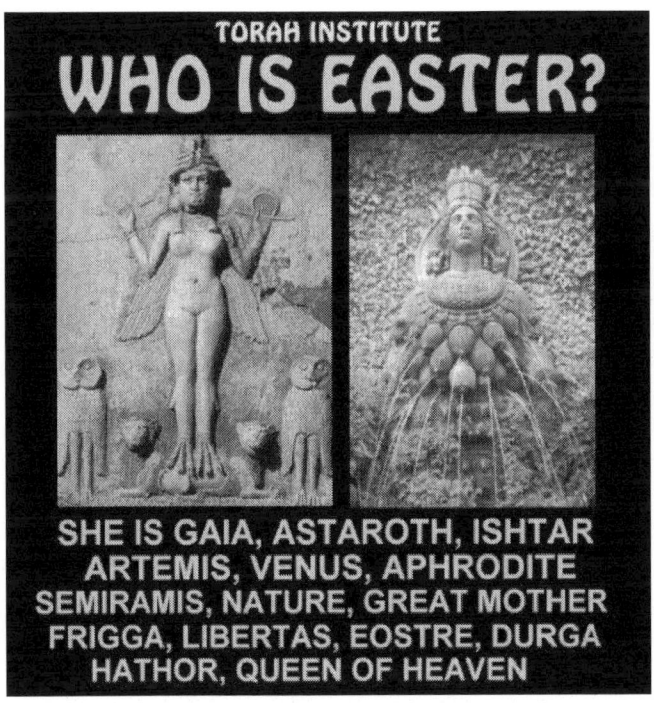

Easter Day - the Pagan festival of the impregnation of Mother Earth by the rays of the springtime sun. Ishtar, Ostara, Astarte, Eostre, Asherah, Eastron, Ashtaroth, and other names were used for this Pagan deity. It became adopted to refer to Yahusha's day of resurrection.
Easter is the proper name of the Pagan Queen of heaven. (Google the words: Ashtaroth, Easter)

Christmas - The winter solstice festival, commemorated as the nativity of the sun, re-thought by Dionysius Exiguus in 525 CE, now promoted as the birthday of the Mashiak. Wreaths (wombs), trees (phalluses), tinsel (semen) & balls (testes) were used to observe the sexual aspects of this pagan ritual. The tree was an altar where offerings were placed for the deity (Asherah).
The womb wreaths and trees represented Asherah and Bel. This is a practice inherited from the ancient Canaanites, specifically Izabel (Jezebel). The bel in Izabel is that deity, and BEL in Hebrew means LORD.

Ultimate determination:
Mashiak Yahusha observed none of these practices.
1 Yahukanon / John 2:3-6:
"We know that we have come to know Him if we obey His Commands. The man who says, 'I know him,' but does not do what He commands is a liar, and the Truth is not in him. But if anyone obeys His Word, Alahim's love is truly made complete in him. This is how we know we are in Him: Whoever claims to live in Him must walk as Yahusha did."

Natsarim walk as Yahusha did, and observe the observances He observed, according to the Word of Yahuah. He lived as our example. So, how does it become appropriate for us to ignore all the things He did, and embrace Christmas, Easter, and Sun-day, observances borrowed from pagan cultures?

Will He find the belief on the Earth when He returns?
This brief comparison is intended to expose the darkness and deception that has overtaken the world.

"For you were once darkness, but now you are LIGHT in Yahuah. Live as children of LIGHT (for the fruit of the light consists in all goodness, righteousness and truth) and find out what pleases (Yahuah). Have nothing to do with the fruitless deeds of darkness, but rather expose them." - Ephesians 5:8-12

Find out what pleases Yahuah, your Creator.
Obedience is praised if it fits traditional norms, but condemned if it fits Scriptural instructions. Scripture is divided, and a division exists between the Hebrew / Yahudi (Jew) and the Gentile Christian in terms of what is to be obeyed or ignored in the Torah, based on this difference. So, in their teachings, there is not one body of believers, although this will be denied by most.
The word **Christianity** is not found anywhere in Scripture. Why do we pretend it is? Encyclopedias tell us it is a *religion*, and that it was founded by *Jesus Christ*. It was really founded by Simon Magus, and his tomb is under the altar in St. Peter's Cathedral at Rome. No follower of Yahusha ever taught us anything about Sun-day, Easter, Christmas, popes, nuns, holy water, sacraments, or any separation of Yahusha's body into a priesthood and laity. We are ALL priests on level ground with one another, and He is our High Priest. If you are studying something, and embrace it as a way of living, shouldn't you search it out completely and find where its roots lead? If the root is good, then the fruit it bears will also be good.
Christianity is a usurper, and a religion without Hebrew roots; it grew from pagan Greco-Latin roots.

WHAT DO THE FESTIVALS MEAN?

The Redemption Plan of Yahuah is shadowed in festivals during the year. These show us "the way" Yahusha is redeeming His bride.
They are found at Lev. 23 & Dt. 16.
One of them is Yom Kafar, Judgment Day.
Yahusha Himself, and Peter and Paul, reveal the Day of Judgment (by fire) that is still ahead of us.
The book of Revelation begins with the statement,
"I was in the Spirit on the Master's (kuriakos) Day" in order to reveal future events to the assemblies. It is only confusing because our slumbering teachers fumble with the meaning of words in their context.
By not feeding the sheep "every Word that proceeds from the mouth of Yahuah,"
the sheep remain unprepared for the day set by Yahuah to remove the weeds (Acts 17:30-31).

HE HAS SET A DAY

"Truly, then, having overlooked these times of ignorance, Alahim now commands all men everywhere to repent because He has set a day on which He is going to judge the world in righteousness by a Man whom He has appointed, having given proof of this to all by raising Him from the dead." - Acts 17:30-31

Download the complete article for free: click here
A DAY IS DESCRIBED AT YUAL (Joel) **2**
A DAY OF EVIL (PROV. 16:4)
A DAY OF DARKNESS (YUAL 2:2)
A DAY OF BURNING (MAL. 4:1)
A DAY FOR REAPING THE WEEDS (MT. 24:28)
THE EAGLES ARE THE REAPERS ON A FUTURE YOM KAFAR
AND IT CONCERNS THE FALL APPOINTED TIMES
ACTS 27:9, LEV 23:27

Do the Word!
The redemptive shadows reveal so much for us.
Remember, without obedience (outwardly showing what we believe, the works), our belief is dead. Yaqub (James 2:14-26) is not talking about animal blood, but obeying the instructions most are taught are a way of evil.

Anguish Among Races
All nations are the people of the book; Yahuah told Abrahim he would father multitudes of peoples. They were spread among the guyim like fine seeds. Those foreigners joined to Him, and who obey Yahuah's Shabath are welcome to His qodesh mountain. Foreigners will be given a name (renown) better than those indigenous peoples (See YashaYahu 56). Wake up, yes, but be gentle, kind, and loving as you share Yahuah's Covenant of kindness, otherwise we are working against ourselves, and Yahuah, the Maker of all of us.Torah is a mirror, a reflection of our behavior, not our skin. Yahuah does not look upon outward appearances, but the heart. White, black, yellow, red, or brown; put yourself beneath others, not over them.
www.fossilizedcustoms.com/mirror.html

Who will hear the cry of the Natsarim?
Yom Teruah (day of the shout) is the 1st day of the seventh month. It begins at sunset where you happen to live, arriving this year on September 29, 2019 and extends until the following sunset. Those seeking understanding should be listening in quiet contemplation, and be in awe of what is casting the shadow of these unfulfilled redemptive feasts of the seventh month. A shout from a shofar is the warning reminder that in ten days Yom Kafar (day of covering) is coming, the Fast mentioned at Acts 27:9.

The Roman calendar month of September is named for the Latin word *septem*, meaning *seven*. The Roman calendar ignores the real months, or make sense of what to call them. The words septem (7), octo (8), novem (9), and decem (10) reveal a only a small glimpse of the nonsense people live by.

Those seeking understanding are realizing their teachers are the reason for all the confusion. Arcane hooey has been inherited from our fathers, and those who are wise are leading many to uprightness. The wicked will not understand, but the wise will understand.
www.fossilizedcustoms.com/redemption.html

How people became entangled in the rapture theories, and the main models are quickly explained in a short youtube video, Two Resurrections. Link:
https://youtu.be/nC8EdGZD6Zs
A very easy-to-understand explanation; Scripture tells it straight.

The Caves Of Doom For Christianity?
The *Dead Sea Scrolls* will eventually be shown to the world. They were in the 11 caves because the Name of Yahuah was written on them, but the Jesuit Scroll Team has not released the scrolls they believe to be dangerous to their teaching authority. The Vatican Library, Ecole Biblique, and the Rockefeller Museum has several of the writings of the first Natsarim as they were originally written, in Hebrew. Anyone can Google the writings of the circus father, **Epiphanius**, and read of his admission to meeting one of the Natsarim in his time, and said he saw the Hebrew scroll of MatithYahu, as it was originally written in Hebrew. Everyone should do this research. Which is the more probable Name of our Mashiak, Yahusha, or Jesus? There is no letter "J" in the Hebrew, nor is their a "J" in Greek, nor is there a "J" in Latin. The name Jesus is not the true Name, because Yahusha is the true Name. Can anyone prove the Name Yahusha is false? It's easy to prove Jesus is false, I just did: no letter J existed until

less than 500 years ago. The "sus" component is "horse" in Hebrew, and "pig" in Latin. In Hebrew, he-Soos means "the horse." Sus is spelled JEZUS in Poland, and is a hail to ZUS. We've been fed lies from our fathers (YirmeYahu 16:19).
www.fossilizedcustoms.com/deadseascrolls.html

CAVES of DOOM (Video description)
The reason the Dead Sea Scrolls are a threat to all Christianities concerns the Name the teaching authorities do not want you to see, say, or even know about.
The world will know Yahuah's Name.
Pastors are scrambling to defend their position they've chosen, but all they have to do is accept the Truth, and nothing but the Truth. Until they repent, Yahusha will not allow them to believe and call on His one, true Name.
www.fossilizedcustoms.com/deadseascrolls.html

How many animals would it take for mankind to be cleansed of all sins against Yahuah's Covenant once and for all? Would it require us to offer all of the animals in the entire world, or would that still fall short of the required number? Ask the Temple Mount Faithful the big questions, like why they want to re-start animal sacrifices again, after Yahuah made it clear to everyone how much He hated it, and offered His own blood to purchase us (Acts 20:28).

When we see Yahusha coming back to wipe-away the reign of Babel, kings will shut their mouths, for that which they have not been told they will see; and that which they had never heard they will understand.

Are you still fiddling around with Halloween?

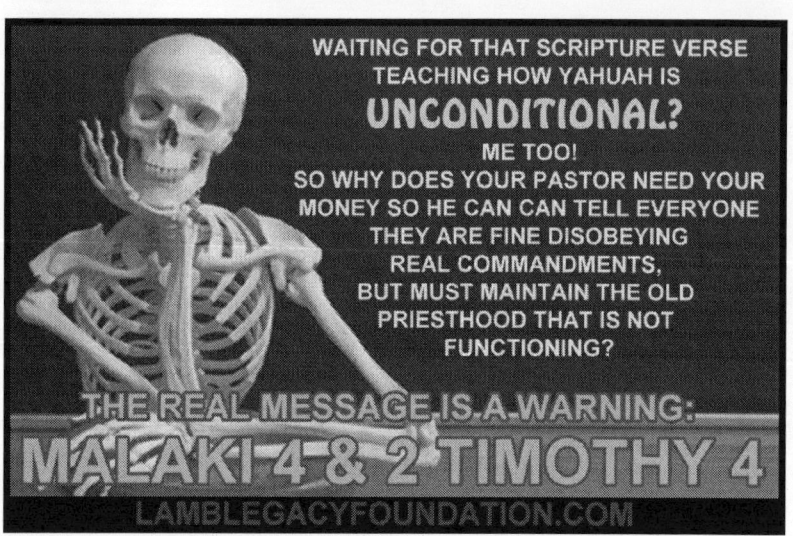

Psalm 91 - Because We Know His Name

To overcome the works of the adversary, teach the Torah of kindness (love). Many believe it is heretical to memorize, obey, and teach others to obey the Ten Commandments. If obeying the Words of Yahuah is not good, what distinction is there to make when the reapers come to take out the weeds from among the wheat? At our immersion, we are sealed as the property of Yahusha, calling on His Name to deliver us, trusting in His blood as the perfect offering for our sins. We pledge to obey, with His help. Psalm 91:14-16 describes why He will deliver us, and gives insight into why so many resist receiving Truth.
They've been paralyzed by the darnel, wheat's evil twin.
http://www.fossilizedcustoms.com/leaven.html

Footsteps of Peace

12 students of Yahusha were given an assigned mission (Mt. 10:5), and told not to go into any town of the gentiles (guyim) or the Samaritans (Shamarunim). Finding the lost sheep of His flock was at the top of His list, but YashaYahu 49:6 shows this was only the beginning of a global plan still to be unfolded.

He has breathed on His last Natsarim today, and we are activated soldiers to restore the breach and paths to walk in. Mt. 28:19, YashaYahu 56:4-8 give us the wider view of Yahusha's mission, but His first Natsarim were told to take the message to Yisharal first. Later we discover it is for the Yahudim first, and also for the Hellenists (Romans 1:16). Yahusha is drawing all mankind to Himself, and His Name is growing more magnificent in all the arets through His last Natsarim. The Arabs are Eberim (Hebrews, descendants from Eber). Many of those imprisoned by the Shiva/Hindu/Islam Nimrod thing are learning, and that is amazing. I'm a redman (Cherokee), and many of the tribes of Yisharal landed in North America on ships during the reign of Shalumah (Solomon). The thoughts and plans of Yahuah are so vast, they are unfathomable. Our inner thoughts are far more capable of getting us disinherited by our Father Yahuah than our skin color, or DNA mixture. The human heart is where the sickness dwells, and the last Natsarim are rising in the power of Yahusha to tear apart all the strongholds imprisoning the minds of all who will hear His voice in us. I was a selfish wretch until He came into me and cleaned-out the filth, and He is still working on me. BTW, thank you for the time you've given to reading this reply. May you always walk in Truth, and share Yahusha with every nation and tongue, and leave footsteps of peace on the hearts who listen to Him speaking through you.

A day begins at sunset, or sunrise?
Act 27:27: "And when the fourteenth night came, as we were driven up and down in the Adriatic Sea, about midnight the sailors suspected that they were drawing near some land."

Act 27:33: "And when day was about to come, Paul urged them all to take food, saying, "Today is the fourteenth day you have continued without food, and eaten none at all."

Please notice that Paul was including the evening prior to the daylight portion of the 'Fourteenth Day.'
More? Scripture reveals the Truth of every controversy:
www.fossilizedcustoms.com/day.html

WHAT REDEEMS US?

Yahusha's blood (Acts 20:28) has purchased us. There was no one named Jesus on Earth 2000 years ago. He only has one Name, and it's Hebrew. Is Yahusha not His Name? This is the real question teachers are facing as their flock brings them many questions to answer. The world was turned upside down by the Name, Yahusha, spread abroad by the first Natsarim. It's already happening again by His last Natsarim, the first-fruits group who have not denied His Name, Yahusha. Acts 20:28 tells us the Ruach ha Qodesh shed His Own blood to purchase us. Yahusha is the Spirit living in you Who guides you into all Truth, but only if you belong to Him. His Spirit is given to those who obey Him (Acts 5:32).

Masoretic Mutilation

Yahuah's Word is for all to hear, but it has been altered in that His Name has been molested. Aduni is a word, however it is not His memorial Name, the four vowels yod-hay-uau-hay. The proof they added to the Eberith language (written in the Aramith script) is in front of everyone constantly. The niqqud marks the Masoretes added during the 8th to 12th centuries are not seen in the Dead Sea Scrolls, or any other texts until they invented them out of their imaginations. The Eberith script is bursting out of the prison men have built, and it's putting Yahuah's Name on the lips of the nations again, just as He told us it would (Psalm 102:18, Psalm 118:26, YirmeYahu 31:34).

Mt. Karmal (Karmal means "Alahim's Vineyard")

The issue is the same as AliYahu faced at Mt. Karmal. People have been deceived by their teachers, and those who learn

the Truth become responsible for it. If Jesus, Krishna, Elmer, or Bel are what people are taught, but the real and only Name given among men is Yahusha, what then? Acts 4:12 is a certainty, however there was no one calling on Jesus when Luke wrote it; yet that is what our teaching authorities have led everyone to believe. The last Natsarim are here, and we have to say the same message as the first Natsarim said. Yahusha is coming soon, but Jesus will never show.
www.fossilizedcustoms.com/transliteration.html

The Message of AliYahu
The witnesses of the last days are Natsarim, and YirmeYahu 31:6 predicted we would appear. We guard Yahuah's Name and His Word. As witnesses, we are saying Yahuah is Alahim, and Yahuah is Yahusha (meaning "I am your Deliverer"). The nations (guyim) that do not call on His Name are discussed at YirmeYahu 10:25 & Psalm 79:6, among many other texts concerning those who reject Yahuah. The last Natsarim are very real, and we do not speak our own words, but those of Yahusha. His reign is coming, and we have to warn every person of the message of AliYahu (Mal. 4:1-6). Revelation 12:17 gives a clear account of how our witness will be responded to: "And the dragon was enraged with the ashah, and he went to fight with the remnant of her seed, those guarding the commands of Yahuah and possessing the witness of Yahusha Mashiak." -Besorah Of Yahusha Natsarim Version (BYNV Kindle Edition)
www.fossilizedcustoms.com/yahusha.html

What Is His Name, Can You Tell Us?
What does Isaiah / YashaYahu 42:8 tell us the Name of our Creator is, considering the context of that interesting statement? Please analyze this from the Interlinear so everyone may see what was done to the Word to arrive at the correct answer.

The readers are welcome to examine the BYNV English translation of Proverbs 30 in the photo.
It's asking the same question; What is His Name?

Seven Sacraments - Mind Control Of The World Order

The greatest power over the nobility was for the circus to withhold the *sacraments* from them if they did not do what they wanted.

What if someone told you the seven sacraments were made up, and a delusional operation established to give credibility to the priesthood of Anglican, Roman, and Eastern Orthodox Catholicism? Would that statement offend you, or awaken you to reality? Psychologists use *triggers* to awaken latent memories deep in the mind of their patients. Natsarim are here to help tear down every false reasoning (stronghold) out of its place with the power of Yahusha, if a person is willing to

accept Him as their only Ruler, and trust in Him alone to guide them into all Truth.
He wrote the book, and is calling us all to believe His Words. The Truth will set you free from all outside influences over your mind. Get to the Truth quick, the world order is about to be removed from existence. Yahuah is coming to reign.
The reign of Babel is about to fall. A new video is being planned soon, called The Message of AliYahu - based on the text of Malaki 4:1-6. Have you read that yet?

Can Sacraments Help Save You? Sacraments are the beast's primary means of control, wielded by the great harlot, and are nothing more than the imaginary incantations of a sorceress. To keep the Nobility (2nd estate) in-line, the Clergy (1st estate) withholds the imaginary sacraments until they follow orders. The control is paper-thin, and the world economy is resting on all the fertility festivals everyone pretends are real. Babel (World Order) cannot be fixed or reformed, all one can do is come out of it by ignoring it. Those obedient to Yahusha hear Him saying, "Come out of her, My people;" and this will cause all the merchants to wail, because no one will buy their merchandise anymore, just as we see written at Revelation 18.

Redemption Plan (without animals or sacraments)
We trust in Yahusha's blood He shed for our crimes against His Covenant. Demons believe Yahuah is One, and also believe He shed His blood to purchases us (Acts 20:28), but this belief must be perfected with obedience (Yahudah / Jude 2). We must repent (turn back, turn from our crimes), or we will perish. If we believe and obey (Acts 5:32), we will receive Yahusha's indwelling Spirit, and He will guide us into all Truth. If we abide in His Word, we are truly His talmidim, and will know the Truth, and the Truth will set us free. The old covenant was the animal blood offered through the old

priesthood (Heb. 8:13), and was placed next to the ark, written on a scroll (sefer; see Dt. 31:26).

If we offered-up every living thing on land and sea, it would not redeem a single person. But if we obey His Word (the eternal Covenant He wrote in stone), trusting in Yahusha's perfect offering, our heart (thoughts and perspectives) is sprinkled with His blood and we no longer desire to disobey. We no longer live, but Mashiak lives in us. Our belief is perfected by our obedience, and how we show our belief. The one not obeying His Commandments does not know, or belong to Him.

www.fossilizedcustoms.com/redemption.html

NIV & NASB PREFACES WILL TELL YOU

The need to "call" on the Name is referenced at Yual (Joel) 2, Acts 2 & 3, and Acts 4:12. The teaching authorities have lulled the world into a deep sleep by adopting the Christograms, codes, mysteries, and every imaginable sort of delusion to keep the masses away from the message of their Deliverer. Malaki 4:1-6 leave us with a 400-year silence in heaven to emphasize how important that message is. Our deliverance is sure, but only if we have place our trust in the One Who is our Deliverer. They removed His Name so we would not know His Name, nor what He desires us to obey. The NIV preface proves they removed the Name of our Deliverer.

> **NIV - PREFACE**
>
> In regard to the divine name *YHWH*, commonly referred to as the *Tetragrammaton*, the translators adopted the device used in most English versions of rendering that name as "L ORD" in capital letters to distinguish it from *Adonai*, another Hebrew word rendered "Lord," for which small letters are used. Wherever the two names stand together in the Old Testament as a compound name of God, they are rendered "Sovereign L ORD."
>
> Because for most readers today the phrases "the L ORD of hosts" and "God of hosts" have little meaning, this version renders them "the L ORD Almighty" and "God Almighty." These renderings convey the sense of the Hebrew, namely, "he who is sovereign over all the 'hosts' (powers) in heaven and on earth, especially over the 'hosts' (armies) of Israel." For readers unacquainted with Hebrew this does not make clear the distinction between *Sabaoth* ("hosts" or "Almighty") and *Shaddai* (which can also be translated "Almighty"), but the latter occurs infrequently and is always footnoted. When *Adonai* and *YHWH Sabaoth* occur together, they are rendered "the Lord, the L ORD Almighty."
>
> As for other proper nouns, the familiar spellings of the King James Version are generally retained.

Natsarim are teaching everyone to obey the Word (Yaqub / James 1:22), not just hear it . With Yahusha's indwelling, we can discern the way He walked, and we imitate Him in every way. He guarded Shabath, didn't eat pigs, and went back to work on the first day of the week. Corrected Scriptural misunderstandings in the BYNV translation is a good thing, such as restoring the Name the former translations removed, which they still forbid anyone to use. The NIV and NASB translators attempt to provide an explanation for removing the Name. Would Yahusha teach us to remove the Name, or are we being bequiled by the same liar that tricked us into eating what we were told to never touch? Have I now become your enemy for telling you the Truth? (Galatians 4:16)

The NASB translators tell us the Name is most significant, and inconceivable for anyone to not have a proper designation for *"the Supreme Deity,"* but they still removed it.

> **The Proper Name of God in the Old Testament:** In the Scriptures, the name of God is most significant and understandably so. It is inconceivable to think of spiritual matters without a proper designation for the Supreme Deity. Thus the most common name for deity is God, a translation of the Hebrew *Elohim*. The normal word for Master is Lord, a rendering of *Adonai*. There is yet another name which is particularly assigned to God as His special or proper name, that is, the four letters YHWH (Exodus 3:14 and Isaiah 42:8). This name has not been pronounced by the Jews because of reverence for the great sacredness of the divine name. Therefore, it was consistently pronounced and translated Lord. The only exception to this translation of YHWH is when it occurs in immediate proximity to the word Lord, that is, *Adonai*. In that case it is regularly translated God in order to avoid confusion.
>
> NASB - PRINCIPLES OF TRANSLATION

The old priesthood is obsolete, Yahusha's blood ended it. Christians replaced everything Yahusha practiced with delusional activities from pagans, and pretend "sacraments" are real. Sometimes when a person becomes angry enough, it will wake them up from their dream. Turning away from sin is easy, but most are trained to turn away from the Commandments. Who has annulled the Commandments, and maligned the way of Truth? (2 Peter 2:2)

Sealed By The Name Of Yahusha?
Our lips are being refined to *call* on the Name Yahusha for deliverance, but not by foreign tongues, the grammer rules of men, or speech directions invented by Karaites 700 years after Yahusha walked the Earth. The Greek and Latin alphabets fail us, but the real Eberith letters (without the niqqud marks men invented) are being resisted.

When traditions are challenged by Truth, this is to be expected. The 22 letters (from Alef to Tau) provide all the consonants and vowels we will ever need.
Free download printable tract - Hebrew Phonology from www.torahzone.net

A Karaite sect, the Masoretes (traditionalists), corrupted the phonology of Eberith over the 8th-12th centuries.
We are drawing close to the return of Yahusha. Yahusha's last Natsarim are saying **"baruk haba bashem Yahuah"** - reminding us that Yahusha said we would not see Him again until we said that very phrase. More about this:
https://youtu.be/30eTPH5Yay0

Why So Much Confusion?
Teachers lead us into confusion, and are even divided among one another. To Yahusha, titles and rank mean nothing.
His first Natsarim debated about who would be in charge while He was washing all their feet. He showed us that the greatest among us in His sight is the servant of all. We each perform different functions in the body, not entitled positions over one another. What we do for Yahusha as His servants is part of a far larger operation of His design. Pleasure, possessions, and position are the desires of the world (1 Yn. 2:16), but Natsarim are to desire Yahusha's purposes, not their own purposes.
If we obey and teach His Word, we will know Him, and His purpose for our lives. This is how we know we know Him: we obey His Commandments, and walk exactly as Yahusha walked.
"And by this we know that we know Him, if we guard His commands. The one who says, 'I know Him,' and does not guard His commands, is a liar, and the truth is not in him. But whoever guards His Word, truly the love of Yahuah has been perfected in Him. By this we know that

we are in Him. The one who says he lives in Him ought himself also to walk even as He walked.
Beloved, I write no original unfamiliar command to you, but an old command which you have had from the beginning. The old command is the Word which you heard from the beginning."
1 Yahukanon / John 2:3-7 (BYNV)

The dragon's messengers think it is heretical to obey the old instructions, and call those who obey Torah "legalists."

The obedient are not enraged because people are obeying the Commandments and testifying of Yahusha, but it enrages another entity. Let's see who that is:

"And the dragon was enraged with the ashah, and he went to fight with the remnant of her seed, those guarding the commands of Yahuah and possessing the witness of Yahusha Mashiak."
Revelation 12:17 (BYNV)

Because teachers have trained their deluded followers to disregard His Commandments, love has grown cold.
Disobedience is reaping a whirlwind of human misery.
It is impossible to repent, and at the same time continue to sin. The Spirit of Truth leads us to obedience, but a spirit of error leads us away from Truth.

"To the Torah and to the witness! If they do not speak according to this Word, they have no daybreak."
YashaYahu / Isaiah 8:20

How will they hear unless someone speaks to them?
The Name is written in 4 vowels; the "vav" is a modern misunderstanding of what a vowel is, as distinguished from a consonant. It is simply a single letter U, heard in the Hebrew / Eberith phrase, "hallelU Yah" - Josephus (Flavius Yusef) in his War of the Yahudim book 5, chapter 5 v.7 states:

"A mitre also of fine linen encompassed his head, which was tied by a blue ribbon, about which there was another golden crown, in which was engraven the sacred name - it consists of four vowels."
http://www.fossilizedcustoms.com/fourvowels.html

 **TURNED ASIDE TO MYTHS**
NOT BEARING SOUND DOCTRINE
TEACHERS INCREASE CHAOS
WHAT COULD POSSIBLY GO WRONG?

2 TIMOTHY 4:1-6   MALAKI 4:1-6

"Proclaim the Word! Be urgent in season, out of season. Correct, warn, appeal, with all patience and teaching. For there shall be a time when they shall not bear sound teaching, but according to their own desires, they shall heap up for themselves teachers tickling the ear, and they shall indeed turn their ears away from the Truth, and be turned aside to myths."* (2Timothy 4:2-4)

*[sacraments, holy water, transubstantiation, Sun-day, Trinities, celibacy, image worship, popes, nuns, monks, steeples, monstrances, chants, special days, lent, prayers to the dead, indulgences, pilgrimages, stigmatas, Easter eggs, December 25th Solstice birth, etc.]

Who Is Lazarus, and Is He Dead?
Alazar, Lazarus, John:
The Disciple Whom Yahusha Loved
Alazar – Lazarus: The world calls him "John."
It's important to realize that some of the first Natsarim had two or even three names.

The person the world calls Lazarus (Alazar) became targeted for death after Yahusha raised him from the dead (see Yn. 11), and was a young man that Yahusha loved dearly.

So beloved was Alazar, that his "gospel" (besorah) was the only one without the writer's identity directly referred to, and the only one with the account of the raising of Alazar (Yn. 11). The writer refers to himself by the phrase, "the disciple whom Yahusha loved." This is the way we can know who it was that is the writer, by deduction.
He is the younger brother of Miryam and Martha, residents of Beth Anya (poor house, or house of figs).
Alazar was the "talmid whom Yahusha loved," and was charged to look after Yahusha's mother as He hung from the stake (Yn. 19). Miryam was one of the women who discovered the empty tomb, and ran to report it to Yahusha's closest talmidim, one of whom was her own brother Alazar, referred to as the
talmid – the one Yahusha loved (See Yn. 20:2).
Abiding in Yahusha's Word, we are truly His Talmidim.
More: **www.fossilizedcustoms.com/revelation.html**

Lazarus (Alazar) **is ALIVE**
John (Hebrew, Yahukanon): one of the two witnesses?
The identity of the writer of the 4th gospel: LAZARUS! (Alazar)
https://youtu.be/zK_T2Lw9blU

"But Yahuah helped me." This phrase, and all of the rest of Psalm 118, is very personal for me. The Name is rejected by the builders, but those called-forth from the darkness have received a white stone with a Name written on it, and have been given the task to share the life of Yahusha our Deliverer with many peoples, nations, and languages. We are alive in Yahusha, and He lives in us.

UR (IRAN) 2200 BCE
Every man praying or prophesying with his head covered dishonors his head. 1Kor. 11:4
LewWhite youtube channel

How To Identify Counterfeit Teachers

Prophesying or praying with the head covered in any way is a dishonor to our Head. The old covenant using animal blood for atonement required for the High priest to wear a highly specialized head covering called a ***mitsnefet***, a wrapped cloth for hair control held in place by a blue ribbon holding the golden signet inscribed,

"**Qodesh L'Yahuah,**" meaning "set-apart to Yahuah."
(see Exodus / Shemoth 28:36-38)

1 Korinthians 11:4 teaches us about headship. The husband is the head of the wife, who seeks approval from her husband and shows cooperation and agreement with him in every matter. Yahusha is the head of every man, and when praying or discussing Scripture (prophesying), does not cover his head. Although thought to be an act of humility, a man

dishonors his Head (Mashiak) if he prays of prophesys with his head covered. Yahusha is our High Priest, and the testimony of Yahusha is the Spirit (breath) of prophesy. Yahuah told us at Yual (Joel) 2:28-29 that He would pour out His Spirit on all flesh in the end times. Through the prophet, Yahuah says sons and daughters will receive His breath, causing many people young and old to dream, see visions, and both men and women will prophesy. At Yn. 20:21-22, Yahusha in His resurrected body breathed on His first Natsarim, saying, **"Receive the Ruach ha Qodesh."** They then could understand the Scriptures by His indwelling, and were enabled to teach what the Word forbids (binds) and what the Word permits (looses). When we obey His Word, He will do the same for all who obey Him (Acts 5:32). Those who will not submit to His Qodesh Spirit will not understand, but those who do will guide many to righteousness. (Danial 12).

Are You Into Halloween?
We are all wrestling - mostly over what to stop doing, and unlearning traditions we struggle to defend. Halloween won't be around much longer, Yahusha's reign will not perpetuate it or any of the Christian holidays. Read 2 Peter 2 and see what it is saying to your heart.
www.fossilizedcustoms.com/halloweenorigins.html

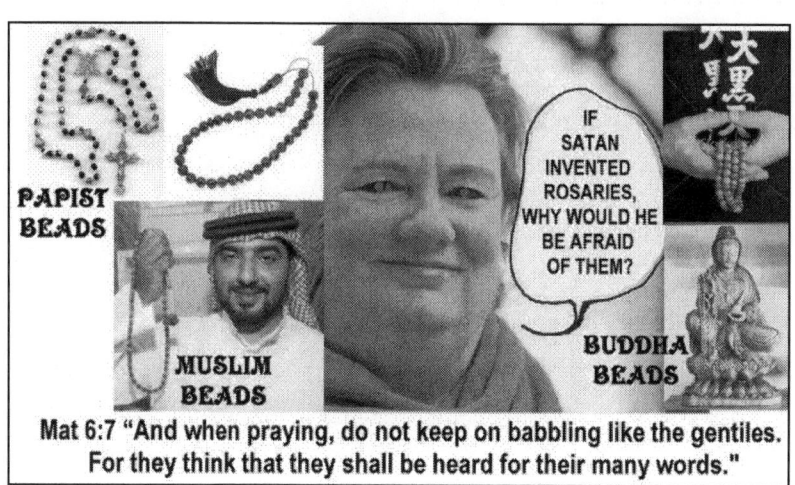

Necromancy is praying to dead people. Hindus, Muslims, and Catholics seem to be unaware of how this practice is an abomination to Yahuah. Rosaries are Shiva's tears, a Hindu item, used by Muslims also because India reached the Middle East by 200 BCE. Catholics received this item at "Fatima," a city named for one of Muhammad's daughters. If beads aren't going to work, how about praying to wood or precious metals, maybe with some candles? No, these are not helping us.
www.fossilizedcustoms.com/allah.html

What About All The New Calendars People Follow?
I've been watching the calendar specialists multiply into several dozen splinters over the decades. We engraft into Yisharal, but the younger brother Afraim is returning, and is very arrogant and resists embracing his older brother. Yahuah only has one schedule for us to all follow (Uyiqara 23, Debarim 16), but teachers have their own understanding of what the words mean. A new month (kodesh) is a period of time (not the Quranic method of a sighted crescent).
A Kodesh is not a new Moon (yerak), but a renewed cycle. The first day arrives unseen, but may be confirmed when enough time elapses for the light of the first day to be fully-built. Most years, some teachers either jump ahead or fall behind by a whole month due to confusion over when the previous year ends, and the new one arrives.
The Yahudim know when the festivals are, and weekly Shabath, but they do not recognize Shabuoth correctly because they have not experienced Zechariah 12 yet. Their count from First-fruits (Yahusha Himself as the wave-sheaf) is off, but that is the only flaw in their thinking I know of. They will see Him coming, and Yahusha will love them in spite of themselves.

"Ani ha Gafen, atah ha Natsarim"
Yahusha said, **"I am the Vine, and you are the Natsarim."** See Yn. 15:5

Yahusha ordered (ordained) His Natsarim to go teach all nations the real Name, and to obey everything He commanded us to obey.

The obedient Natsarim (branches) are not enraged because people are obeying the Commandments and testifying of Yahusha, but it enrages another entity.

Let's see who that is:

"And the dragon was enraged with the ashah, and he went to fight with the remnant of her seed, those guarding the commands of Yahuah and possessing the witness of Yahusha Mashiak." - Revelation 12:17 (BYNV)

The dragon's messengers think it is heretical to obey the Commandments, and they refer to Yahusha's last Natsarim as legalists.

When Yahusha returns, I hope to be found a commandment-guarding legalist with the dragon in hot pursuit; how about you?

NATSARIM ARE VERY REAL

We were prophesied to appear at YirmeYahu 31:6, and Revelation 12:17 explains we are the first-fruits, enraging the dragon because we obey the Commandments of Alahim and

hold the Testimony of Yahusha. Christianity was born at Alexandria, Egypt, and reinforced by the authority of Rome beginning at Nicaea in 325 CE. The Natsarim were based at Antioch just prior to the destruction of the Temple, and had to hide themselves from the Christian Magisterium for over 1000 years. We were forced to dwell in the hills and valleys, and called Passagans, Albigensians, Waldenses, and Huguenots. We are proclaiming the Name of Yahusha around the world as His envoys. A Catholic website mentioned this author's name, and I attempted to answer their questions about the Natsarim, but was blocked permanently.
I saved the discourse we had up to that point.
My book *Last Natsarim* also has this discussion:

CATHOLIC FORUM TOPIC: NATSARIM
A BRIEF CONVERSATION BETWEEN A JESUIT AND A NATSARI

Because my name (Lew White) came up on a Catholic forum, I registered to respond to several questions being asked about what they referred to as *"the cult of the Natsarim."* This is the entire, but brief, interaction I had with the Jesuits. You will find their final response very interesting.
Catholic forum topic: NATSARIM
The original post on the forum asked the question:

Jesuit question to the forum:
Has anyone heard of the cult of the Natsarim? What are it's core beliefs and how does it relate to Jewish and Christian religion??

(This is my original reply to the question, because my name was mentioned in the forum as being in a cult, the Natsarim):

My reply:
The term **NATSARIM** is used to describe the original followers of Yahusha of Natsarith at Acts 24:5. The term *Christianos* is found 3 times in the Greek, but the term was, in that time, a Greek term of scorn, used in a list of other scornful labels at 1 Peter 5:8.
The Hebrew/Yisharali followers of Yahusha did not call themselves by a **Greek** term, but were at first **called** *Christianos* at Antioch, according to Acts 11:26. If you look up the term **cretin** you will find it is traced back to the original Greek, *Christianos* a scornful term used in that time to describe a simpleton, or an idiot. The term later was adopted by those at *Alexandria*, and propelled by the headmasters of the Catechetical School of Alexandria.

For every weird accusation there is a logical, truthful answer; my reputation has been commonly smeared, but so was the "cult" called Natsarim in the days of the first followers - Acts 28:22:

"And we think it right to hear from you what you think, for indeed, concerning this sect, we know that it is spoken against everywhere." (a sect is a subset or variation from a larger group or culture, hopefully motivated to remove erroneous teachings)

Jesuit reply:

But am I to understand you are yet another group of Judaisers?

My reply:
Catholics refer to those who rest on the Sabbath by the term *Judaizers. Heresy* is the strongest accusation one group will accuse another one of. Strong (and deadly) disputes arise between groups who share similar, but not identical beliefs. Sunni and Shia are similar, but not identical, and so each group considers the other heretics.
Since the 12th century, the **Natsarim** (aka Huguenots, Waldensians, Pasagians, Cathars, Albigenses, Ebionites) kept the Commandments as written (including the true Sabbath, not Sun-day), and were brutally attacked by German, French, and Bohemian armies for centuries, long before the *Reformation.*

The WIKIPEDIA ENCYCLOPEDIA **states:**
"The Roman Catholic Church declared them heretics — stating the group's principal error was **'contempt for ecclesiastical power'**.
The *Waldensians* were also accused by the Catholic Church of teaching 'innumerable errors'."
JUDAIZER is the label often used today for those who obey Turah, however at Galatians 2:14 it specifically was over adult male circumcision - Paul confronted Peter over this point, and it was finally decided on as recorded at Acts 15, with Yahusha's brother James (Yaqub, aka Jacob) presiding over the Natsarim assembly (he was the Nasi, or president of the Natsarim). If we obey the true Sabbath, and teach love, obedience to Turah, we are accused of being Judaizers, and thus heretics. The fruit of the tree is the way you determine the kind of tree it is. We Natsarim teach love, which is the outcome of guarding the Commandments. The bad fruit, centuries of extermination, including before the Inquisition

existed, must be placed in another divisional camp, which will be judged by Yahusha, not me or any other Natsari.
We are to love, teach, and obey; not judge.
We are labeled heretics because we love the Commandments, and shun the Nicolaitane *"ecclesiastical powers."* We still love our enemies, and don't kill them. We hold no power, nor pursue it. Yahusha is our Head, we are His body. The fruit identifies the tree it hangs on.

Jesuit reply:
Lew, You did not answer my question. **You just lost credibility and earned a report to the forum masters.** I believe that you are proselytizing ...You are preaching.

My reply:
I'm not preaching, I'm addressing the question. Specifically, the question was: *are we a sect of Judaizers?* The *context* is often misunderstood, since a Judaizer referenced from Galatians 2:14 pertains to circumcision, which is the book Paul wrote addressing the topic of circumcision. Catholicism condemns those who **rest on the Sabbath** as Judaizers, and they even refer to the Sabbath in their decision from the Council of Laodicea in 365 in 59 laws, Canon #29:
"Christians must not Judaize by resting on the Sabbath, but must work on that day, rather honoring the Lord's Day; and if they can, resting then as Christians. But if any shall be found to be Judaizers, let them be anathema from Christ."
One would have to concede that Yahusha and all His followers would be anathema according to this dogma. The law even makes reference to *"the Sabbath,"* so they acknowledge it is a **real day of each week**. The council orders that **work be done on the Sabbath**. Who would teach this to be pleasing to Yahuah?
Romans 6:16 tells us the one we obey is the one we serve. You did not know this?

Jesuit reply:
Do you regard the Natsarim as the true Messianic Judaism and do you strictly follow Turah Law?

My reply:
There is no such thing as **Messianic Judaism.** This term was invented to describe those who may be of the tribe of Yahudah, but also practice rabbinical Judaism, based on Talmud as well as Turah, began by a rabbi - or exalted one - named Akiba, 2nd century. Rab is a Hebrew root meaning *chief*, as in *Rabshakeh, chief cup-bearer.*
The true faith of the followers of Yahusha involves belief in His atonement (by His blood sprinkling our hearts, or inner spirits), *and walking in the way He walked; in Turah.* We are obliged to go, teach all nations what *we* were commanded to obey, and that is easily found at Ex. 20, Lev. 11, and Lev. 23. It's not difficult in the least, and in fact a very light *yoke* (teaching). There's only one rabbi, Yahusha. BTW, there's no such thing as a *Palestinian* either.
The word *Palestine* is based on the term *Philistine*, and is a Latinization. Philistines no longer exist as a people anywhere. **Natsarim are very real however.**

Jesuit reply:
So you reject the Oral Law (Talmud) as being transmitted by G-d together with the Written Law (Turah)? That would be similar to Karaite Judaism. Do you then consider the Natsarim the only true Christians, apart from using the term itself?

My reply:
There is no such thing as an *oral law*. As for our similarities with Karaites, the TaNaK is the basis of the revelation of Truth; but unlike them we also embrace the writings of the Brith Chadasha (referred to as the "New Testament" by Christianity). We overcome *strongholds* (mental fortresses of

errant beliefs) by the indwelling of the Spirit of Yahusha Who guides us into Truth and discernment.
He gives His Spirit to those who obey Him (Acts 5:32).
We are not a *religion*. We are guardians of
the **Name** (Yahuah) and His **Word** (Turah), which He has exalted above all (see Ps. 25:14, Ps. 138:2).
This forum asked the question, **what are the 'core beliefs' of the Natsarim?** - you're communicating with one of the Natsarim now.

Jesuit reply:
Thank you for your informative responses. One more question: do you believe in the divinity of Jesus? I assume you don't believe in the Trinity; am I correct?

My reply:
Yahusha is Yahuah, as He revealed to Philip (Yn 14:9). *"Have I been with you so long, and you have not known me Phillip? He who has seen Me, has seen the Father..."* Sorry, but there's no "trinity" revealed as a teaching in Scripture. It came along much later as a part of the creed developed pertaining to "baptism" (immersion in water, our pledge of a good conscience toward Yahuah, and our commitment/marriage/joining to Him). The Spirit is Yahuah, but since Yahuah is the **same Person** as Yahusha, there is but ONE Person, not three -- unless you can produce a text of Scripture that actually teaches there are *three persons*.
(Acts 20:28 says the Ruach ha Qodesh purchased the assembly "with His Own blood.")
We are keen to discern between "exegesis" and "eisegesis." Our *wineskins* are new, and only accept the teaching authority of Yahusha. Old wine (men's traditions) will not remain where the "new wine" (Yahusha's Word/teachings) have been accepted.
The Light drives away the darkness, overcoming it completely. If Yahuah were truly **3 persons**, He would have surely told us.

Most Pagan religions involved 3 (**Baal Shalishi** - "3 LORD"); all derive from Babel: **Nimrod, Tammuz, & Semiramis**.
BAAL is Hebrew for "LORD," so we don't substitute His Name for "LORD" either. These are just some details that may be interesting, I'm not intending to upset anyone.

Jesuit reply:
Your account has been locked for the following reason:
Trolling, agenda posting
This change will be lifted: Never
The site also removed each posting where they conversed with me, and all my responses.
This is the webpage where I have preserved this conversation:
http://www.fossilizedcustoms.com/catholicforum.html

What Happens When Our Body Dies?
Yahusha raised Alazar and several other people from the dead, and even stated that they are asleep, not dead, but if they stay asleep, they will perish.
People are up walking around in a kind of sleep also. All the while, they pretend (dream, imagine) to believe what others around them are pretending. they think they are awake. They dream their lives away as the traditions of men swoon their thinking patterns around pagan ideas from Nimrod Land. It's no wonder they remain asleep with all the domes, chakra symbolism, sacraments, holy objects, fertility patterns set-up around the year, steeples, and mystagogues to guide them into the mysteries.
We pursue knowledge about things we cannot possibly fathom, and waste our time listening to mystics who claim to know.
Life and death are always our choice. Draw close to Yahusha, and you will know Life and Truth, and not have to worry about these things. Stay away from religion (men's traditions), and live the way Scripture tells you to live. It's appointed that we

die once, but to die twice is totally unnecessary.
www.fossilizedcustoms.com/religion.html

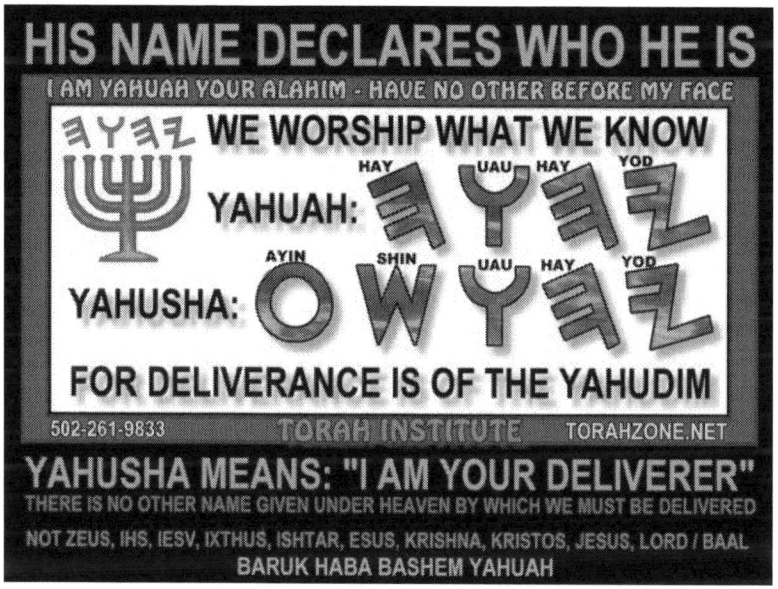

The Tetragrammaton-Watch Continues
The Vatican Library allowed photos of some seferim (scrolls) dating to the later Middle Ages to be released. They are copied in Aramith script. Because they were found in the Vatican Library, it's likely these Masoretic scrolls were seized from a synagogue the Inquisition had raided and / or destroyed. The niqqud marks were invented almost a Millennium after the oldest DSS began to be placed in jars there or at Masada. There is no substantial evidence of a consonant sound "V" in the Tetragrammaton.

A headmaster at the Catechetical School of Alexandria, Clement (died 215), attempted to transliterate the Tetragrammaton in the Greek letters **IAOUE**.
These are all vowels, as we are finding to be true today.
The V sound as we know it today is less than 500 years old, probably far less. The Greek letter upsilon became the Latin shape V, but sounded as our modern U. The uncial (capital)

Greek letter upsilon matches the shape of the Hebrew letter in the Name: Y. This Greek upsilon lost the lower stem as it was adopted into the Latin script. This Y shape is the third letter in the Name, misunderstood to be "W" or "V" in sound. They call it waw or vav today, but neither are accurate.

Clement of Alexandria shows the Tetragrammaton was pronounced "Iaoue" in all Greek vowels. The "ou" in "Iaoue" is a Greek diphthong, thus "Ia(ou)e" is composed of 4, not 5 Greek vowels. No consonants using lips, teeth, or tongue to the roof of the mouth is indicated.

What Is His Name, And What Is His Son's Name?

Those who are convinced the third letter of the Name uses a consonant (Jehovah, Yehovah) need to explain why Yusef Ben MatithYahu (Flavius Josephus) said he saw four vowels, and Clement of Alexandria used Greek vowels to transliterate the Name (IAOUE). Were they incorrect?

Although the Name in the four vowels is used in the writings of Truth almost 7000 times (more than any other single word by far), we still have different understandings of how it sounds. The papal bull of 2008 outlawed using the Name entirely. Where are we, Mt. Karmal? There's very little disagreement on Ben, Babel, Yusef, Miryam, Aliyahu, Yarusha, Alisha, Yashayahu, Netanyahu, or even the hypocorisma (diminutive form) "YAH" we see at Ps. 68:4, yet when we read "I am ? ? ? ? , that is My Name" - (see YashaYahu / Isaiah 42:8), hysteria breaks forth. What is His Name, and what is His Son's Name? How should we pronounce Yahuah, Yahusha, in the clean lip He promised to restore to us (ZefanYah 3:9)?

EBERITH SCRIPT
WRITTEN RIGHT-TO-LEFT
NO SPACES BETWEEN WORDS

YOD-HAY-UAU-HAY:

People may tell you they know something about the Hebrew script because of a school they attended.
The more we listen to all the voices out there, the more confusing it gets on almost every detail.
Hebrew was originally written with no spaces between words, which helps explain why Philip heard the Ethiopian reading YashaYahu aloud in his chariot (Acts 8:26).
The rules men have invented for how to transliterate the language is only rivaled by the confusion

resulting from their interpretations. Only Yahusha can open our mind to understand what He inspired in those who wrote the words for us, and He will inspire you if you shut out all the other voices.

His thoughts are alive in the words, and all the other voices are straining to get the message without Him.

They've made their rules, and insist that everyone else live by them. **https://youtu.be/nrnyBAalhYM**

Yahusha is the same Person Who met Mushah at the bush in Midian, Exodus 3. When Mushah asked "what is Your Name?" the first response is AHAYAH ASHER AHAYAH, "I will be Who I will be" but the Name is still to be shared in the following verses, revealed to be the four vowels giving us the sound Yahuah. When Yahuah became Yahusha, the added suffix SHA (shin-ayin) reveals a functional aspect to suggest deliverance. The suffix (SHA) in AliSHA and YaruSHA do the same. The suffix is from another root, YASHA (yod-shin-ayin), the first part of YashaYahu, only in that case the modifier is a prefix using the whole root. The four vowels in Yahuah use a root HAYAH (hay-yod-hay) to give the meaning of "exist" or "I am," also a part of the word AHAYAH, "I will be Who I will be." Yahuah is explained to Yahukanon (Yahuah is kindness).

At Rev. 1:18 Yahusha claims to have been dead, yet is alive forever, and 1:8 states "I am He Who was, Who is, and Who will be, Al Shaddai." He claimed to be the the One. Al Shaddai means to be mighty overwhelmingly so. Yahuah means to self-exist eternally (past, present, future). When Clement of Alexandria used Greek letters, he used all vowels, and kept only four if you think of the (ou) as a diphthong (dipping of the tongue to create more mouth cavity): **IAOUE**. This produces the phonology we use across the world so the whole world can say His Name in the last days: YAHUAH.

Hebrew uses compound words, prefixes, roots, and suffixes. The word / name "**Rab**shaqeh" means "**chief** cup-bearer," or "chief butler." Rab means chief, rabi means my chief, and shaqeh is exactly how James Bond would order his martini, not stirred (shaqeh really does mean to shake, and the Rabshaqeh's job involved adult beverages). Don't let the rule-makers on the Internet ruin your joy and understanding of Yahusha's wonderful language.

Tel Arad
Videos of street preaching are being put up on youtube making it seem the true descendants of Yaqub (aka Israel) can be identified as those who have black skin. They also believe slavery to be the common heritage of the blacks everywhere, as if only the black skinned people of history fit the description. They also teach Yahusha is only the Redeemer of Yisharal, i.e., black skinned people. They tend to overlook the mixed multitude of others that became a nation in the deliverance from Mitsrayim. Even if one assumes only black skinned people were true Hebrews, it all begins to fall apart because Yahuah also refers to the foreigners (guyim) who guard His Shabath. They will be given a name better than sons and daughters (YashaYahu 56), so whatever race you may be, it won't even matter to Yahuah. Yahuah says just the opposite of what all the white, red, black, or yellow bigots are saying. Scripture doesn't contradict itself, but faulty interpretations turn the Word into wormwood. Notice YashaYahu / Is. 49:6:
"He says, 'It is not enough for you to be My Servant, to raise up the tribes of Yaqub, and to restore the protected ones of Yisharal. I will also make you a light for the guyim, that you may bring My deliverance to the ends of the arets." I am Cherokee in part, indigenous dwellers of this land, and my ancestors came on ships sent long ago during Yisharal's colonization period under king Shalomoh. To think skin matters to Yahuah is arrogant nonsense. The Natsarim are followers of Yahusha, and are made up of all racial backgrounds. People have a problem, but it is in their hearts, not in their skin or DNA.

Yisharal, Yasharal, or Israel?
The commonly understood transliteration "Israel" is from the letters yod-shin-resh-alef-lamed: YISHARAL.

This word doesn't have the root YASHAR (straight, upright) in it, and yet we are often seeing it transliterated YASHARAL. The first letter yod is a prefix adding the meaning "to" - joined with the root SHAR (rule, ruler). The suffix letters alef-lamed (meaning lofty one) shows we co-rule with Alahim.

The word Yisharal literally means *"to co-rule with Alahim."*

"Wrestle with El" is how most define the meaning of the name "Israel."
There's more to the encounter than what we've inherited from our teachers about the new name given to Yaqub at Barashith / Genesis 32. Yaqub wrestled with Yahuah, lost the match and was permanently disabled, but kept pursuing the identity (the Name), seeking to know all he could about Him. The root SHAR (rule, prince) can be understood as "to overpower" with Alahim after he wrestled with Yahuah. Yaqub was given a new name looking forward to all who overcome (rule) with Yahuah. The prophet ZakarYah (4:6) alludes to the real source of our overcoming:
"This is the Word of Yahuah to Zerubabel, 'Not by might nor by power, but by My Ruach,' said Yahuah Tsabauth."
Besorah Of Yahusha Natsarim Version (BYNV)

Lexomorphosis:
a condition when tricky letters seem to be morphing from vowels into consonants, placed there by suggestion.
YashaYahu 52:5-6 tells us those who rule over His people make the "howl." The context is discussing His Name, go look at it and see.
Until we change our perspective, we will never know how we look to Yahuah:

"Elder and highly respected, he is the head; the prophet who teaches falsehood, he is the tail. For the leaders of this people lead them astray, and those who are guided by them are swallowed up." YashaYahu 9:15-16

The leaders are highly respected, but will face a harsher judgment, so we have to choose to please men, or please Yahuah. One day we will know if we made the right choice. The written letters as they were recorded are one approach; the other is to follow rules men have made, and pretend the letters are trickier than we suppose, and a guru is needed to explain them. The rules of men are where everything gets twisted. The schools that teach the rules made up by men all say the same thing, and the crowds are usually wrong because they were misled.

Standing alone, Yah is my final answer, even if the whole world is trained to see something else. Whether Yah is at the beginning, middle, or ending of a word, that's His Name, and no man can bend it.

www.fossilizedcustoms.com/lexomorphosis.html

Our words and actions reveal who we serve, and I admit I am learning everyday, and don't know hardly anything. I am more stupid than most (Prov. 30:2-5). Teachers have tried to conceal His Name, but it is rising up to be known as the waters cover the Earth. Yahusha's Name will never morph into Elmer, Rumples, Twitchy, Jesus, or anything but what it has always been since the messenger of Yahuah appeared to Yusef (Mt. 1:21). The messenger even gave the reason why Yahusha would be His Name. Jesus has no meaning in Hebrew, other than perhaps "the horse" (he-soos).

Yahusha is Yahuah with a suffix, and means "I am your Deliverer." Yahusha quoted Ps. 118:26 when He told us we would not see Him again until we said at Mt. 23:39, "Baruk haba bashem Yahuah." Do I sound like someone who doesn't know Him? He has been my only Teacher for many decades, and I could never deny His Name (Rev. 3:8).

Yahuah bless and guard you; Yahuah make His face shine upon you and show kindness to you; Yahuah lift up His countenance upon you, and give you shalom.

"Let no corrupt word come out of your mouth, but only such as is good for the use of building-up, so as to impart what is pleasant to the hearers. And do not grieve the Ruach ha Qodesh of Yahuah, by whom you were sealed for the yom of redemption. Let all bitterness, and wrath, and displeasure, and uproar, and slander be put away from you, along with all evil. And be kind towards one another, tenderhearted, forgiving one another, as Yahuah also forgave you in Mashiak." Ephesians 4:29-32

1 Peter 4:1-7 & 2 Peter 2:1-6 help to show us our Creator's view of our behavior. Yahusha in us pleads with us to be restored to favor to Him. We show our belief by our obedience, and our belief is shown in our words and actions. Let's do all we can while we live to show the world it is no longer we who live, but Yahusha lives in us. He is perfecting us, and we know Him, if we guard His commandments.

GLOSSARY
Hebrew Transliterations & Definitions

This is a partial listing of Hebrew / Eberith transliterations and definitions. Meanings are determined by the *context* of the word. How a word is used in a sentence helps us discern how to apply a proper definition. A pitcher can mean more than one thing, and Hebrew words can too. At the end of this glossary is a *letter comparison chart*. The **context** supplies a word's meaning in a sentence. A common error of many students and teachers is to consult a concordance and select a definition on a whim. The meanings a word may have must not be applied mindlessly without taking the context into account.

Ab, Abba [alef-beth] .... Father, male head of household, strong protector

Aban [alef-beth-nun] .... stone

Abrahim .... Abram or Aburamu (exalted father) renamed by Yahuah: Abrahim - father of Guyim or father of multitudes

Adam .... Man, mankind, human, humanity, Earthling; created with a shared essence / character with Yahuah, in order to

rule over creation; depending on the context, it can also mean red, or soil

Adun, Aduni .... Master, or Aduni: "my master."

Afraim .... Second son of Yusef, received blessing of first-born. His name means *fruitful.* Commonly spelled *Ephraim*

Al, Alah .... Al, Alah, Alahim are pronouns meaning the mighty, high, or lofty one. The plural ending can refer to the majesty, or power of the One. Commonly we see the spelling **El, Eli,** or **Elohim** due to the subtle distortion of vowels invented by the *Masoretes,* Karaite **traditionalists.** The first letter is **ALEF**; an **A**, not an **E**. Al is pronounced *ALL*. Yahuah has hidden the sound of His original Speech in a most unexpected place: Arabic-Hebrew. Those who are concerned that EL, and ALAH have been used as **proper nouns** by pagans should distinguish the difference between a **NAME**, and a **clean Hebrew word** that is a **pronoun**. Other cultures have picked up many clean Hebrew words and turned them into names, such as Aman, Adon, and Molok. When not used as **names**, these terms are authentic, clean words. The decendants of Abrahim through Yishmaal were not attacked and carried into all the world, but continue **to utter the old form** of many Hebrew words, since they ARE **Hebrews**. They refer to their mighty-one as **allah**, which they know is not a name, but simply means god, as they explain it to English-speaking people today. The term itself **is original**; but **their** allah is not **our Alah, Yahuah**, since **their** allah does not have a son, and they do not obey Yahuah's Covenant. Many other words are preserved on the Masoretes. Arabic/Hebrew from *the other side of the family* preserves the original sound of words such as Abram, Daud, Yusef, Yaqub, Aishah, dam, Iason, etc. The Arabic/Hebrew word for mother, *um*, closely resembles the modern Hebrew *em* [vowel-trouble again]. The Arabic/Hebrew for father, *ab*, is more correct than the modern

Hebrew, **av**, since there was not a letter "**V**" in ancient Hebrew (Eberith, and later referred to as Yahudith).

Am, Ama [alef-mem] Mother, female term, one giving birth, nurturer; EM [ayin-mem] means *people.* AM means *mother*

Aman .... 3 Hebrew letters, alef-mem-nun: **AMN** [AMAN] Meaning: affirmation; *truly, trusted, affirmed, believe, confirm* The femine form is **amanah**, found in Scripture translations as belief, but means trustworthy. Both aman and amanah refer to the idea of being **trustworthy** and **truthful**. It is perfected or shown by **action**, the active belief expressed outwardly. *"Who has believed our report?"* [YashaYahu 53:1] The word believed uses this root AMN to convey belief, and that **belief** is perfected only by **obedience**. The affirmation of our amanah (belief in, or integrity) is shown in our behavior, or how we live it out. If we do not live by the Word we claim to believe, our belief is dead. We show our belief by our works, the way we live, approved by the Word of Yahuah. This is the fruit of Yahusha who dwells in us, giving us His Mind. This word is **not in any way** related to the Egyptian deity AMEN or AMON RA. The word **AMON** is the **Greek form** of the Egyptian word *YAMANU*, which meant the *hidden-one*. There is no relationship or contextual connection between the Hebrew use of the word **AMAN** with the Greek or Egyptian languages. People are hearing things that aren't there, therefore they are being deluded / mesmerized by malicious teachings. Proverbs 14:15 tells us how a simpleton believes everything he hears, but a prudent person watches over their steps.

Arets .... Earth, soil, land

Aish, Ashah ... Man, Woman - male: *aish*; female: *ashah*

Asherah ... tree idol plural: Asherim Seen today in the Christmas tree, a phallus depicting gonads (orbs) and semen (tinsel)

Astoreth ... plural of Astoreth, Philistine deity; aka Astarte; equivalent to Eostre, Eastre, Easter, Isis, Ishtar, and others.

Baal, BEL .... Lord, Aduni, owner; a word adopted as a proper noun (name) for the Kanaanite storm deity BEL, in Hebrew it is spelled BETH-AYIN-LAMED plural: **Belim**

Behemah .... A beast, living creature; plural: *BEHEMOTH* The plural may refer to a single beast of a great size. Certain plural endings in Hebrew pertain to quantity, but in some cases the quality of strength or size. Also used as a metaphor for the principalities controlling and ruling mankind (clergy, nobility, and laity), given power and authority by the dragon. A more modern term is **beast**: a giant monster (World Order).

Beital .... Bethel, meaning *house of al*

Besorah .... Message, testimony, report

Farah .... [pe-resh-ayin-hay] usually seen as the Greek form, *Pharaoh*, a title for the ruler of Mitsrim (Egypt). The word means *great house* in the Egyptian language. This political and religious ruler was believed to be a deity, Horus, the son of Osiris. These reflect patterns adopted from Babel where Tammuz was the son of Nimrod, who was believed to be the "son of the Sun." It explains how people believed in reincarnation, and Egypt's fascination with embalming mummies, and equipping them for their passage into the next world.

Farat .... A river commonly known by its Greek form, Euphrates

First-fruits .... This is a shadow or outline using the waving of barley during the week of Matsah, or Unleavened Bread. Following Passover, we see the sign of Yunah because Yahusha's resurrection is the redemptive shadow showing Him to be the First-fruits. It's really not about barley at all, the barley was simply the shadow; Yahusha's resurrection is the reality.

Guyim .... Plural form of guy, meaning Guyim, Guyim. The word means nation or nations, often referring to the foriegners we are commissioned to teach the Name of Yahuah and His Covenant. Those responding will engraft to Yisharal by pledging themselves to the Covenant in immersion; then they are to be treated the same as native-born. There is no dividing wall; the same Turah applies to all.

Hekal .... Temple, Shrine *The House built by Shalomoh, destroyed by Babylonians, rebuilt after return from Babel under governor, NekemYah*

Kanukah .... Dedication (aka Chanukah, Hanukkah)

Kerem .... Vine, vineyard, or garden
The Hebrew word for vineyard is *KEREM*. This word is spelled with three letters in the original Eberith (Hebrew) script: KAF – RESH – MEM (please see letter chart on last page) Yahusha is the KEREM (Vine), and we are His NATSARIM meaning *branches, watchmen, or guardians*

Kodesh .... Renewed month, cycle, *period of time* (see QODESH)

Kohen .... Hebrew word for priest; plural *kohenim* The meaning is friend, worker, minister, server. Cognate words include kahuna, kahin, king, koehn, kohn, cohn; revealing how the word is synonymous with many statements about us becoming kings and priests under Yahusha, our Kohen haGadol (the High Priest)

Kuram-Abi: [2 Kron 2:13] ,,,, *A Tyrain man of the tribe of **Dan** filled with wisdom and skill. In their drive to promote Reason as the highest goal, modern Masonry's Adepts refer to this man as they seek vengeance against 3 allegorical conspirators they claim slew Huram: government, religion, and private property – Marxist philosophy embracing Secular Humanism, situation ethics, athieism, and communism [New World Order, New Age, the worship of Reason]*

Lailah .... Night, darkness

Lui .... The name of the father of the tribe of priests, *Lui*; plural form *Luim*, commonly seen as LEVI, LEVITE; Aharon and Mosheh were *Luim*

Malakim .... Messengers; singular form: malak, "angel"

Mayim .... Water, waters; a component of **shamayim**

Miqara .... Proclamation; root *QARA*, to proclaim, or call. MIQARA is another phonetic spelling, seen as UYIQARA, *"and he called."* The **Karaites** derive their name from the meaning. The Arabic term **quran** is derived from the Hebrew word ***qara***.

Mishkan .. Temple, Dwelling Place

Moed .... Appointment; plural form: moedim

Molok .... Kananim / Muabim deity also known as Rephan, Kemosh [to Amonites], Kiun, Tophet, etc.,. Children were offered alive to pass through the fire as offerings to this abomination

Mosheh .... Hebrew spelling: mem-shin-hay: *draw-out*

Nashim .... Wives

Natsarim .... Plural for Natsar. The original followers of Yahusha were the sect of the Natsarim (Acts 24:5). The word means watchmen, guardians, also used to mean branches. We are branches of the teachings of the Root.

Nazir .... An oath of separation for a specific purpose and duration. It also refers to the person under the oath. This is an entirely different word than Natsar.

Nefesh .... Breath, blast, living spirit, life-giving essence, cognate with nehash (breathe), and nekash (hiss). Often translated *soul,* inner being, strong man, psyche.

Qodesh .... Peculiar, special, precious, exceptional, distinctive, treasured above all, esteemed. (not KODESH, the word for month)

Rab, Rabbi .... Chief; rabbi means my chief, or *my exalted one.* The Rabshakah (chief of the princes) mentioned at 2 Kings 18:17 was an Assyrian official sent against Yerushalom, also mentioned at YashaYahu chapters 36 & 37. We have no chief but Yahusha.

Ruach ... Breath, wind, breeze, also known as spirit

Sefer .... a *book* (Latinized form: cepher)

Shabath [shin-beth-tau] . . . rest, cease, complete shalom, the 7th day of each week, a sign forever between Yahuah and His people. It is the test given by Yahuah to determine who will obey Him, and is the sign of the eternal Covenant.

Shabathuth .... Plural form of shabua: *weeks*. The event memorialized as the marriage Covenant between Yahuah and Yisharal. The Eternal Covenant is annually observed on the 50th day after First-fruits, and is always on the first day of the week, the *"morrow after the seventh Shabath"*

Shalomoh .... Peaceful, Man of peace, son of Daud

Shabua .... Week, from root *sheba*, seven; plural form: *Shabuoth* (weeks)

Shamash .... Servant; context may refer to the visible object called the Sun, or the adopted name for the deity pagans called on to worship the Sun. The context supplies a word's intended meaning in a sentence. A common error of many students and teachers is to consult a concordance, and select a definition on a whim. The meanings a word may have must not be applied mindlessly without discerning the context.

Shamayim .... Skies, heavens. The word means lofty, and the second part of the word refers to "waters" – the waters from which all creation began with.

Shaul .... Usually seen as SHEOL; Abode of the dead, **the grave**, commonly called hell, meaning *hole* - not the same as the Lake of Fire, **Yam Aish.** The same Hebrew letters [shin-alef-uau-lamed] also spell a word sounding the same (a homonym), Shaul. The context of will identify it as a proper noun (name). Shaul was the 1st king of Yisharal, whose name means "asked for." Although words may be spelled and sound exactly alike, we must use their context to determine what they mean in a sentence.

Shamar .... Watch, guard. We often see the idea softened to the English word, "keep." We guard and watch over Yahuah's Torah carefully, we don't just "keep" Torah.

Shamarun .... Known as Samaria, a hill in the northern area of the land used as a watch station. The word is based on the word *shamar, to watch or guard.*

Sukah, Sukuth .... Shelter, shelters, temporary dwellings

Sus .... Hebrew spelling *samek-uau-samek* – meaning *horse*

Talmid .... Student, pupil; plural form, *talmidim*

Turah .... Instruction; plural form *Turoth*

Tsabauth .... Armies; *tsaba* (army) + plural suffix, *uth*

Tsedek .... Upright, obedient, righteous. Tsedekah is obedience in practice, literally the living-out of the Word of Yahuah.

Tsitsith .... Tassels (purplish-blue in color, see Num. 15, Dt. 22). They are worn on our garments to remind us to obey the Instructions of Torah always. The Hebrew word also applies to the place on a plant where fruit will appear.

Tsiun .... Literally, the location of the City of Daud. Usually spelled Zion, Sion, or Tsiyon. The meaning is signpost, from the verb root *tsuh*, command or charge. Tsiun is the place of authority from which the ruler of Yisharal is identified to reside, and possesses authority to dispense the full code of law.

Uriyah .... [Uriah] Yahuah is my Light.

Yahuah .... 4 vowels: **yod-hay-uau-hay**. The Personal Name of our Creator, meaning: I will be there; *I was, I am, I will be*. Greek: Tetragrammaton (4 letters).

Yahusha .... Name of Mashiak, means: *Yah* (I am) *your Deliverer*

Yam, Yamim .... Lake, sea; *yamim*: seas

Yam Aish ... Lake of fire, place of permanent, utter destruction; this is the second death

Yerak .... Moon (the visible object of the Moon) Yereku is the city people today call "Jericho," named after this Hebrew word for Moon.

Yisharal .... Ruler with Alahim **Shar** means prince, ruler; seen today in terms such as sheriff, sharif. The word is built around the root **shar**, with the single letter **yod** as a prefix, and the **al** as a suffix: Y ("to") + SHAR ("rule") + AL (Alahim) means *"to rule with Alahim."* This elect group is often referred to in Scripture as the bride, or ashah, of Yahuah, the one body in Covenant with Him, into which foreigners **must** graft in, or perish without any hope. All who accept the Renewed Covenant through the covering of Yahusha's blood (trusting in His offering, not the blood of animals), must be immersed as the outward sign of their pledge / commitment to obedience. This seals them as Yahusha's elect for the Day of their redemption. By learning Yahuah's Covenant of love, every person is convicted of transgressing His instructions. Yahusha's perfect offering of His own blood redeems completely. There remains to more offering for sins. The hand-writing that was against us is wiped clean (the list of our sins). They are forgotten, and His blood redeems us. Through the process of being convicted in our heart that we need Him, we repent (turn back), and pledge to obey Yahuah's instructions in His power as we call on the Name of Deliverance for the forgiveness of sin: Yahusha. He is our Rock and our Redeemer.

Yom, Yomim ... Day, days; it is often and exact measurement of a night/day cycle, but the context may express figurative meaning, as "in those days," or when the Sun rises. Sunset is the end of each "day," and a new one begins in darkness, as it was in the beginning on the first day. "There was evening (darkness), and there was morning (boker), the first day."

Yusef .... Son of Yaqub, father of Afraim (Ephraim) & Menashah; distorted by letters & vowels of gentile languages to become "Joseph"

Zunah .... Whore, cult / shrine prostitute

"This is written for a generation to come so a people to be created praise Yah." Tehillim - Psalms 102:18

Repent - for the Reign of Yahuah draws near!
The Message (Besorah) **of Yahusha; did you hear it?**

ABOUT VESSELS AND WINE

OLD WINE:
The teachings of men are traditions inherited passed-down over generations. These man-made customs commonly dominate behavior, taking precedent over the Words we are to live by written by the Creator. They are a heavy burden we can remove easily by choosing to stop listening to them, recognizing their teachings are nothing to Yahuah; they are only arrogant nonsense someone made up for people to follow. The old wine is the **leaven** of men's teachings. We must be strong and courageous, and obey Yahuah. It's a choice between their teaching authority, or Yahuah's.

NEW WINE: The teachings of Yahusha, without human traditions mixed in. New wine is pure Truth, and cannot be in the presence of old wine. The old wine will conflict **with the new, having the excuse "The old is good enough."**

WINESKIN: The heart, mind, or inner person that receives teachings, accepting both Truth and error based on personal choices. A renewing of this mind, or wineskin, is given when a person **surrenders** their mind, along with the old wine, to Yahusha. The new wine would burst the old wineskin, and cannot be in the presence of the old wine. The wineskin is the receptacle, or vessel, we call our mind. It is our inner heart. Unrenewed by the Ruach of Yahusha, it is a mind of the flesh. A mind of the flesh does not, and cannot, obey, and repels pure Truth (the new wine). Receiving the Mind of the Ruach, one's vessel (wineskin) understands the Scriptures, and the will of Yahusha, so the person pants to obey, knowing the thoughts of Yahusha. They have received a love for the Truth, and their hearts (wineskins) are circumcised by Yahusha. They see the world and its condition, and sin, for what they are in Yahusha's perspective. Yahusha has given them His Mind, and they see everything as He does.

HOW TO GRAFT-IN
IMMERSION IS YOUR PLEDGE
Immersion is our outward sign of a good conscience toward Yahuah, and our "dipping" (baptein) represents our **circumcision**; carefully notice Kol. 2:11,12:
"In Him you were also circumcised, in the putting off of the sinful character, not with a circumcision done by the hands of men, but with the circumcision done by Mashiach, having been buried with Him in immersion (baptism) **and raised with Him through your belief in the power of Yahuah Who raised Him from the dead."**
An infant cannot possibly be considered capable of knowing what is happening. Immersion is an act of your own personal will; You covenant personally with Yahusha, and it is your **heart** (inner spirit, the seat of your will) that He circumcises with a **love** for His Turah. Our immersion is the moment we personally enter into the renewed Covenant with Yahusha, our Maker, when **He** writes His Turah on our hearts, explained at Jer. 31:31-33, and quoted at Hebrews chapters 8 & 10. It's operation is explained in Romans chapters 6,7, & 8. We become a citizen of the commonwealth of Yisharal. According to Rev. 12 & Rev. 14, we are sealed in His Name, and enjoin to Yahuah as a member of the sect of the **NATSARIM** (see Acts 24:5, 28:22), the **first-fruits**. We are those who do 2 things: we obey the **Turah,** Commands of Yahuah, and hold to the Testimony of Yahusha. His Natsarim are guardians or watchmen, and we guard His **Name** and His **Word**.
OUR PLEDGE IS A CHOICE between LIFE & DEATH
Dt. 30:19 & 1Yn 5:11-13:

"And this is the witness: that Alahim has given us everlasting life, and this life is in His Son. He who possesses the Son possesses life, he who does not possess the Son of Alahim does not possess life. I have written this to you who believe in the Name of the Son of Alahim, so that you know that you possess everlasting life, and so that you believe in the Name of the Son of Alahim."

Yahusha circumcises our hearts (minds) Kol. 2:11-13:

"In Him you were also circumcised with a circumcision NOT MADE WITH HANDS, in the putting off of the body of the sins of the flesh, by THE CIRCUMCISION OF MESSIAH, having been buried with Him in IMMERSION, in which you also were raised with Him through the belief in the working of Alahim, who raised Him from the dead. And you, being dead in your offenses and the uncircumcision of your flesh, He has made alive together with Him, having forgiven you all offenses."

The act of immersion is evidence of our circumcision, the outward sign or act of our belief, indicating the **circumcision** (cutting) **of our heart**. Men boasting in one anothers' flesh are missing the point. If we have received Yahusha's Ruach, we are His, and **He** has circumcised our hearts with a love for the Truth, a love for His **Turah**. If you have been circumcised with a circumcision not made with hands, you're done. Nothing **you** can do can improve on what Yahusha has done. This is how we can "obey from the heart." When we love Him enough to obey Him, He will write His Turah on our hearts. Those who will not obey Him will not receive His Ruach (Acts 5:32).

"He who turns away his ear from hearing the Turah, even his prayer is an abomination." Proverbs 28:9.

The Turah (Word of instruction) is oil, also called living water. It is the MIND of Yahuah (His **will** living in us). It is the Mind of **the Ruach** of Yahusha, often called the Spirit. The Turah is inseparable from the Spirit of Yahusha, and it is **"living and active"** (Heb 4). Our heart is our **lamp**, the component within each of us (often called our mind). Our **heart** is what needs the **Living Words** to be poured into them, like **lamp oil** to our **lamp**, or **new wine** for our **new wineskin**. Stephen called the Turah given at Sinai the **Living Words**. Most reject them because they are guided by malicious shepherds, ravening wolves, masquerading as messengers of light.

"Listen to Me, you who know obedience, a people in whose heart is My Turah; do not fear the reproach of men, nor be afraid of their insults."
See YashaYahu / Is. 51:7.

THE PLEDGE OF A GOOD CONSCIENCE
1Pet. 3:15-22:
"But set apart Yahuah Alahim in your hearts, and always be ready to give an answer to everyone asking you a reason concerning the expectation that is in you, with meekness and fear, having a good conscience, so that when they speak against you as doers of evil, those who falsely accuse your good behavior in Messiah, shall be ashamed. For it is better, if it is the desire of Alahim, to suffer for doing good than for doing evil. Because even Messiah once suffered for sins, the obedient for the unobedient, to bring you to Alahim, having been put to death indeed in flesh but made alive in the Ruach, in which also He went and proclaimed to the ruachs in prison, who were disobedient at one time when the patience of Alahim waited in the days of Noah, while the ark was being prepared, in which a few, that is, eight beings, were saved through water, which figure (example) now also saves us: **immersion – not a putting away of the filth of the flesh, but the pledge of a good conscience toward Alahim –** through the resurrection of Yahusha Messiah, Who, having gone into heaven, is at the right hand of Yahuah, messengers and authorities and powers having been subjected to Him."

CAN WE PERFORM OUR OWN PLEDGE ALONE?

Yes, we can, because all that matters is that Yahusha hears our words. Nicolaitanes don't like this, so most people are baptized into a denomination, and the only one that utters a word is the malicious shepherd dipping the person into the water. We can use any body of water; an ocean, stream, lake, pool, or bathtub. An elder is not **required** to be present, and if one is, it is only what we utter that matters. Don't worry, there *are **witnesses**;* an abundance of *rejoicing **malakim*** (messengers). Our immersion represents the death of our old self and its inclination (character). We cannot clean-up or improve ourselves, but rather we acknowledge our filth and sin to the only One that can take our burden away forever, and *change our heart.* We go to Him broken-hearted and humble, and accept the cleansing of His perfect blood to cover our sins against His Covenant. Belief is shown by our obedience.

Heb 11:6: **"But without belief it is impossible to please Him, for he who comes to Alahim has to believe that He is, and that He is a rewarder of those who earnestly seek Him."**

First, we must believe that He **exists**, and we must know that "sin" is any transgression against His Turah (1 Yn 3:4). Admitting that we have transgressed against Him, we turn-back (repent) with all our heart and pledge to ***obey*** (stop sinning). We are now ready to enter into His Covenant, which is a **relationship**, not a religion. We go to the water to identify with Him in His death, burial, and resurrection from the dead. We pronounce our belief in His atonement for our sins through His shed blood (the perfect offering for sins), and **call** upon His **Name** for our deliverance. We accept with a love for His Turah (Truth, His Covenant), and **promise to obey Him as would a bride her husband** -Read YirmeYahu 31, Heb 8, Heb 10. We accept His love, and give Him *our* love; and this is love:

2Yn 1:6: **"And this is the love, that we walk according to His commands. This is the command, that as you have heard from the beginning, you should walk in it."**

Acts 4:12 **"And there is no deliverance in anyone else, for there is no other Name under the heaven given among men by which we need to be saved."**

The Name given to all mankind for deliverance is **Yahusha**, meaning "I am your Deliverer." The *Name*, not the *Names*, indicates that it is Yahuah that became flesh, becoming our Deliverer, and the Name Yahusha identifies Him in the role of Deliverer, giving all honor to Yahuah in the Name of Yahusha as Deliverer (see Phil. 2).

Mat 28:18-20: **"And Yahusha came up and spoke to them, saying, 'All authority has been given to Me in Heaven and on Earth. Therefore, go and make talmidim of all the guyim, immersing them in the <u>Name</u> of the Father and of the Son and of the Qodesh Spirit, teaching them to guard all that I have commanded you. And see, I am with you always, until the end of the age.' Aman."**

With each immersion, Yisharal increases in number. You may have been formerly Gentile, but after immersion you are no longer *gentile* (guyim: the nations).

Read Eph 2:11, and all of Eph 2 & 3, in context.

Exo 12:49: **"There is one Turah for the native-born and for the stranger who sojourns among you."**

Once immersed, we are no longer strangers or foreigners, but **adopted children**. When we read the 10 Commandments, we should feel convicted of sin; we then repent by choosing to live by them, accepting the Covenant by being immersed. We are then sealed for the day of our redemption because we call on Yahusha's Name, and walk in obedience in His power.

TRANSLITERATIONS

	6,823	216	2	1
	YAHUAH	YAHUSHA	YAHUSHUA	Y'SHUA
HEBREW	ᴣYᴣƱ	OWYᴣƱ	OYWYᴣƱ	OYWƱ
ARAMAIC	יהוה	יהושׁ	יהושׁו	ישׁו
GREEK	IAOUE	IHSOUS		
LATIN	IEHOUAH	IESU		

AT HEBREWS 4 AND ACTS 7 THE SAME GREEK LETTERING IS USED FOR "JOSHUA" AND "JESUS" - IHSOUS
THIS IS CONFIRMATION BOTH WERE CALLED YAHUSHA IN HEBREW
TORAH INSTITUTE

The translation with the restored Name and phonetically clear transliterations of the Hebrew words in this glossary is pictured above, and available from amazon.com.

> "This is written for a generation to come,
> so a people to be created praise Yah."
> Tehillim - Psalms 102:18

REPENT
[Reverse your direction]
for the Reign of Yahuah draws near!

The Message (Besorah) **of Yahusha; did you hear it?**

Millions of families have been feeding on myths and lies mixed with Scripture for their entire lives, and those teaching them are paid to teach them. Those teachers will remain just as deceived as they have been, unless they go to them and ask them the questions found in this little book.

None of the questions in this book will harm the Truth, but any one of them will destroy the lie that has been used to conceal the Truth. With the armor of Yahuah, and the fruits of the Living Alahim Who dwells in your mind, you may remain confident and assured that you are firmly established on the Rock of our deliverance. If you are not immersed and have never called on the Name of Yahusha for the forgiveness of your crimes against Him, you are not wearing the armor of Yahusha, and cannot bear the work ahead of you.

Take the first step, by studying the Ten Commandments. They will show you they are His seeds of the coming reign of Yahusha, and teach us all how to love Him and one another.

THIS IS THE LOVE
"For this is the love for Yahuah, that we guard His Commands, and His Commands are not difficult, because everyone having been begotten of Yahuah overcomes the world. And this is the overcoming that has overcome the world: our belief. Who is the one who overcomes the world but he who believes that Yahusha is the Son of Yahuah? This is the One that came by water and blood: Yahusha Mashiak, not only by water, but by water and

blood. And it is the Ruach who bears witness, because the Ruach is the Truth."
1 Yn. 5:3-6 BYNV

IMMERSION IS YOUR PLEDGE
Admit you have broken this eternal Covenant, and pledge to obey His Word from this point on. As you enter into a body of water, tell Him you will obey His Word, and trust in His perfect blood to cover your transgressions, the blood of the Lamb of Yahuah. Immerse completely, calling on His Name to deliver you, and you give your life to Him as His servant forever.
He will help you by writing a love for His Covenant on your heart (mind), enabling you to see the ugliness of rebellion as He does. Yahusha means, "I AM YOUR DELIVER."

COVENANT OF LOVE

1
I AM YAHUAH YOUR ALAHIM
HAVE NO OTHER BEFORE MY FACE

2
YOU DO NOT BOW TO IMAGES

3
YOU DO NOT CAST THE NAME OF
YAHUAH YOUR ALAHIM TO RUIN

4
REMEMBER SHABATH
GUARD IT AS QODESH

5
RESPECT YOUR FATHER & MOTHER

6
YOU DO NOT MURDER

7
YOU DO NOT BREAK WEDLOCK

8
YOU DO NOT STEAL

9
YOU DO NOT BEAR A MALICIOUS
WITNESS AGAINST YOUR NEIGHBOR

10
YOU DO NOT COVET YOUR
NEIGHBOR'S WIFE, HOUSE, FIELD,
SERVANTS, ANIMALS, OR ANYTHING
BELONGING TO YOUR NEIGHBOR

ᐊYᒣZ
I AM YAHUAH, THAT IS MY NAME
LOVE ME AND GUARD MY COMMANDS
LOVE YOUR NEIGHBOR AS YOURSELF
LOVE ONE ANOTHER AS I HAVE LOVED YOU

TORAHZONE.NET   LAMBLEGACYFOUNDATION.COM   NATSARIMSEARCH.COM

The Ten Words above are to become your character because they embody the personality of Yahuah. He ordered us to teach them diligently to our children. The 4th one is the outward sign of the day of rest each week, showing we do not buy and sell on that day, or the 7 festival days we rest from work.

QUESTION: Why do the people who love Yahuah and obey His Torah suffer so much? Kefa (Peter) 5:8-10 explains this.

Another answer is found at Revelation 12:17.
All things work together for good for those who love Yahuah and are called according to His purpose (Romans 8:28). The experience of Ayub (Job) tested the character of everyone around him. The world is filled with comfortable people, and unless they are challenged by pain, persecution, and loss, they would never turn to Yahuah or develop compassion and love. If we suffer, we are being refined and perfected, and to test the hearts of many who may have caused that suffering. All who suffer share in Yahusha's suffering, and YashaYahu 53 describes why the innocent suffer for the guilty. Ecclesiastes is another resource with great wisdom. In the end we are all tested in this mortal life to see if we will obey Yahuah, or place our trust in men. Pledge your life to obeying Yahuah, and He will give you His seal of ownership, and you will see what Psalm 91 means.

TURNING ASIDE TO MYTHS HAPPENS
WHAT COULD POSSIBLY GO WRONG?
CAUSE: 2 TIM 4   EFFECT: MAL 4   FOSSILIZEDCUSTOMS.COM

Merchants And Their Witchcraft
Acts 20:28 says the Ruach ha Qodesh shed His own blood to purchase (redeem completely) us. The Spirit of Yahusha indwells those who obey Him (Acts 5:32).
We call on our Creator as our deliverer by calling Him Yahusha. He is Yahuah, and as our Deliverer we use the suffix SHA at the end of the Name to refer to Him. If we do not obey His Commandments, we do not belong to Him, nor can we claim to know Him. (See 1 Yn. 2:4).
The old traditions of men are as chaff, and the dragon is enraged because people are turning back to obedience to the Commandments of Yahuah, repenting because they are sobering-up from the leaven of men's teachings:
Sun-day; holy water, statues; replaced name; sacraments; praying to the dead / necromancy; special days they made up as "holy" yet not mentioned by Yahuah; teaching Yahuah's

Word, but putting it behind them and not doing His Word; building steeples on every corner in spite of Uyiqara / Lev. 26:1, objects Yahuah hates; always learning, but never able to come to a knowledge of the Truth. Our teachers have led us into confusion. Yahuah our Alahim is One (Dt. 6:4); not three persons - that's Hinduism's influence on mankind, as well as the "4 - levels of interpretation" people keep hearing from teachers. Idolatry drives the economy of the world, just look at the seasonal displays of the merchants, and how silent the pastors are as they struggle to make them relevant with 3-point sophistry. Rebellion is as witchcraft, unrecognized by the simple; but the obedient watches his steps.

IDOLATRY
MANKIND'S MOST PROMINENT ACTIVITY

MANKIND'S DEFINITION
Extreme admiration, love, or revering of something or someone; worship of a physical object or person;

YAHUAH'S DEFINITION
Setting one's thoughts or actions on anything above Yahuah. He gives an example for us from His prophets, such as YashaYahu (Isaiah) 44:16.

IDOL EXAMPLES: politicians / rulers; movie or music idols; statues, pillars, toasting with drinks; prayers to any entities other than Yahuah, spirits, dead people (necromancy, beads).

IDOLATRY
MANKIND'S MOST PROMINENT ACTIVITY

Expressions we hear used all the time in conversations, and the things we run out to buy and decorate with show how invested we are in all the witchcraft, and hardly ever associate them with idolatry: rosaries, steeples horseshoes and rabbits' feet for good luck - bringing trees into our homes to celebrate a birthday, Black F-day, "let's keep our fingers crossed," horoscopes, palmistry, fortune cookies, baking cakes for birthdays, cone hats, toasting, blowing-out candles, wishes, eggs in baskets and rabbits in the spring, sunrise services, giving candy to costumed children on the day of the dead, Valentine's Day gifts, cards, hearts, and using decorations that remind everyone that we encourage the idolatry that drives the world's economy. The golden cup of Babel has caused madness!

DRIVING THE WORLD ECONOMY

Every merchant prospers from the fertility celebrations that hardly anyone perceives because they are all hypnotized from a lifetime of exposure to the traditions handed-down from our fathers to children. **Idolatry** is exactly what Yahusha referred to as **stumbling blocks** at Mt. 18:3-8. Idolatry is taught to children, and passes into each new generation through family bonding.

Yahuah is sending the plagues now, but most people remain clueless to why.
Revelation 9:20
"And the rest of mankind, who were not killed by these plagues, did not repent of the works of their hands, that they should not worship the demons, and idols of gold, and of silver, and of brass, and of stone, and of wood, which are neither able to see, nor to hear, nor to walk. Merchants exploit the wormwood that causes the masses to stay drunk on the idolatrous fertility traditions.

Personally, I have learned a great deal from the training Yahuah has used to shape my heart. I've learned how words can be cruel. They have the power of life and death in them. Words of death often flow from the unredeemed, and even from those who have not walked with Yahusha very long. The longer you walk with Him, the more you become like Him. He is not cruel, so we are not cruel. We can't force love because it is a fruit, not a seed. It comes from Him, the Life of the Root. His life grows and bears His fruit in us. Love cannot be faked, but cruelty is easily seen as the fruit coming from the wicked treasure. Patience and compassion, and above all forgiveness, are expressed in all those who know Yahusha. The mark of the beast can be solved if you have wisdom (Torah).

Revelation 13 is a riddle, and all you have to do is understand what day you cannot buy or sell. The lie has been there all along, and all you need is wisdom to see it. When you receive wisdom, you can see everything as Yahusha does. Are you one us yet?

QUESTION: What is the greatest lesson to learn?
To love Yahuah, and love your neighbor. His Commandments are the seed, and when that seed grows, His fruit is seen in us.

TEACH THEM TO YOUR CHILDREN & GRANDCHILDREN

QUESTION: How do we learn how to love?
Study diligently, and teach everyone around you, to receive a love for the Ten Commandments. Without these, the enemy has you **completely disarmed** in this spiritual war.

The dragon has made these illegal because all who obey them become the enemy. The knowledge of the Truth destroys the lie.

"Yahuah, my strength and my stronghold and my refuge, in the yom of distress the gentiles shall come to You from the ends of the arets and say, 'Our fathers have inherited only falsehood, futility, and there is no value in them.'"
YirmeYahu / Jeremiah 16:19 BYNV

"And besides these, my son, be warned – the making of many books has no end, and much study is a wearying of the flesh. Let us hear the conclusion of the entire matter: Fear Alahim and guard His Commands, for this applies to all mankind! For Alahim shall bring every work into right-ruling, including all that is hidden, whether good or whether evil." Qoheleth / Ecclesiastes 12:12-14

If only you had obeyed My Commands!
YashaYahu / Isaiah 48:18

We will not see Him again until we say:
BARUK HABA BASHEM YAHUAH
BLESSED IS HE WHO COMES IN THE NAME OF YAHUAH – Psalm 118:26
See also YashaYahu (Isaiah) 25:9

How is the BYNV different from other familiar translations?

The following four photos will explain some of those differences.

BESORAH of YAHUSHA
NATSARIM VERSION

You search the Scriptures because you think you possess everlasting life in them. And these are the ones that bear witness of Me. Yahukanon/John 5:39

THE FAMINE OF YAHUAH'S WORD IS OVER

NO MORE HIDING HIS IDENTITY

OUR DELIVERER'S NAME IS ON THE COVER

WHAT THE TEXT LOOKS LIKE:

Mt. 26:17 EVIDENCE OF CONFUSION

PASSOVER: 14th
THE 1ST DAY OF UNLEAVENED BREAD IS THE 15TH

Have you ever heard someone say, *"I just don't understand what I'm reading?"* People are searching for the Heart of Yahusha, but in most translations there are dispensational and Masoretic distortions that block understanding because **His heart** was not in the translator(s).
Respectfully, ignorance of Torah has blocked the understanding of both the translators and their readers.
Footnotes often argue with the text, steering a reader's heart away from receiving the pure and simple instructions to live by. **They are ever learning, but unable to come to a knowledge of the Truth.**
Truth was distorted, causing a famine of His Words.
We Natsarim love Yahusha's **Word**, and His **Name**. The message (**besorah**) of the reign of Yahuah is pouring forth into the world through His Natsarim. In this Natsarim Version, all the blockages to the Truth are removed. The One we **obey** is the one we **serve**.
A servant's **behavior** displays the will of their master.
Our heart is focused on Yahusha's instructions:
   His **Torah** (this is **wisdom**, our **treasure**).
For those curious about readability, here is a sample of the actual text, showing the font style and size:

TEHILLIM - PSALMS 23
₁ ᴀʏᴀᴢ is my Shepherd; nothing do I need. ₂He makes me to lie down in green pastures; He leads me beside still mayim. ₃He returns my breath; He leads me in paths of righteousness for His Name's sake. ₄When I walk through the valley of the shadow of death, I fear no evil. For You are with me; Your rod and Your staff, they comfort me. ₅You spread before me a table in the face of my enemies; You have anointed my head with oil; My cup overflows. ₆Only goodness and lovingkindness follow me All the Yomim of my life; And I shall dwell in the House of Yahuah, for the duration of Yomim! (Glossary defines terms)

Open your favorite translation to Mt. 26:17 and check something right now, if you can. If it says "On the first day of Unleavened Bread," then that translation used the KJV as the primary blueprint to build on, and failed to catch certain errors. The NIV back-pedals the error at Mt. 26:17 in the footnotes. The Greek text has no

BYNV: Besorah Of Yahusha Natsarim Version
An English translation of all 66 books with the restored palaeo-Hebrew Names
Yahuah: ᴀʏᴀᴢ   Yahusha: ᴏᴡʏᴀᴢ

(BYNV tract, page 1 of 4)

word "day" in the sentence, and the word "protos" indicates *prior to* Unleavened Bread. One cannot prepare for the Passover on the "first day of Unleavened Bread." The Greek text has the word *protos*, meaning something is *"near to, before, or prior to."* If one has a *"proto-cancer"* cell, it is **not yet** cancer, but getting there. The festivals of Yisharal were not familiar to Christian translators; but they are to Natsarim. This translation puts many details right, making pure Truth (new wine) easy to absorb into your renewed wineskin (renewed heart).

THE MESSAGE
COMES THROUGH
VERY CLEARLY

TRADITION: A stumbling-block, and when defended, it is also a **stronghold**. The teachings of **men** are "old wine", but the Truth is "new wine." The new and the old cannot be in the presence of the other. Doctrines of men have resided in hearts (old wineskins) for millennia. A renewal of hearts and minds (wineskins) must take place in order to receive the new wine. It's our training that matters.
Even **our speech** needs to have things restored that have been hidden from us. Luke 12:2, 3:
"And whatever is concealed shall be revealed, and whatever is hidden shall be known. So, whatever you have said in the dark shall be heard in the light, and what you have spoken in the ear in inner rooms shall be proclaimed on the housetops."
We know the Name has been hidden: Proverbs 30:4:
"Who has gone up to the shamayim and come down? Who has gathered the wind in His fists? Who has bound the waters in a garment? Who established all the ends of the arets? **What is His Name**, And **what is His Son's Name**, If you know it?" ZekarYah 3 states His Name for all to see.

People are unaware of things carefully planned behind closed doors. The **Masoretes** (traditionalists) invented "vowel-points" to supposedly "lock" the Hebrew words into a uniform pronunciation. *They worked at this from the 7th to the 11th centuries.* Their true agenda was to alter the **vowels** in words so the true pronunciation would be concealed. Notice again, Yahusha's Words above; He refers to something "hidden" that is not "heard", until it is "proclaimed". We see immediately how this would apply to the Name, **Yahuah**. The Name is the **Stone** the builders rejected, and has become the chief cornerstone. Ps 118
The Name is restored in this version, and there are many other restored words to stretch your renewed wineskin. For example, the word "elohim" as traditionally understood, should begin with the letter "a", ALEF. Thanks to the Masoretes, the true letter, "a", is not seen or heard. The true Hebrew word? **ALAHIM**. The first reaction is, *"Uh-oh,* did I hear *ALAH* in there?" This *pronoun*, which

(BYNV tract, page 2 of 4)

is not a name, is more correctly pronounced by Arabs (who are Hebrews) than the modern Yahudim. We have to distinguish their **religion** from their **language** in this case; Abraham knew Yahuah by His Name, but also as Al Shaddai. I've had to accept the Truth of all this, and not ignore it.

It's a simple **vowel-correction** throughout this version. Alef-Lamed is AL, not EL. Working closely with the Hebrew **without the influences of the** Masoretes' agenda restores the **pure lip**.

Yahudim today say AV & EM for **father** and **mother**; Arabs say AB & UM. Arabs name their children Adam, Abram, **Daud**, and **Yusef**. The Arabs were not dispersed into the nations, and have **preserved Hebrew words** well. What happened to their worship practices is another issue entirely.

Yahusha cried out the first verse of Psalm 22, "Ali, Ali, lama sabakthani?" in the Hebrew tongue. He did not say "Eli, Eli." How do we know? Because the Masoretes had not yet corrupted the vocalization with their made-up "niqqud" vowel-markings. This is another tradition we are freed from, removing a huge language barrier, if one's stronghold (thought prison, boxing in a person's understanding) will allow it. This translation is for the next, and possibly the last generation before Yahusha returns. The drought is ending; Living Water is now flowing.

"Then Yahuah will guide you continually, and satisfy your being in drought, and strengthen your bones. And you shall be like a watered garden, and like a spring of water, whose waters do not fail. And those from among you shall build the old waste places. You shall raise up the foundations of many generations. And you would be called the Repairer of the breach, the Restorer of streets to dwell in." (Isaiah) YashaYahu 58:11, 12

Here is the most revealing explanation of what has been going on: "See, days are coming," declares the Master Yahuah, "that I shall send a hunger in the land, not a hunger for bread, nor a thirst for water, but for hearing the Words of Yahuah. And they shall wander from sea to sea, and from north to east – they shall diligently search, seeking the Word of Yahuah, but they shall not find it." – Amus 8:11, 12

The **Living Words** are able to be found among Yahusha's Natsarim. We are His Hekal (Temple, Dwelling Place, His body). "He who **has an ear, let him hear what the Ruach says to the assemblies.**" Rev 2:7 The 7 annual festivals of Yahuah have not been understood by Christianity, nor the Yahudim that have faithfully observed them for thousands of years. This is another case of "whatever is concealed shall be revealed". This is **the first generation** that has comprehended the significance of these "shadows" of things to come for the body of Mashiak. They are redemption shadows, depicting the work of redemption by Yahusha. There are 7 of them, and they are agricultural allegories to illustrate the deliverance of Yisharal: Passover, Matsah, First-fruits, Shabuoth, Yom Teruah, Yom Kaphar, and Sukkoth allow us to see dimly as in a mirror through our observance of these festivals. Festivals are abstractions, or metaphorical ideas about Yisharal's redemption.

Yahusha was born during Sukkoth (also known as Tents, Tabernacles) at

THE ORDER OF THE BOOKS IS IMPROVED IN THIS VERSION. THE LIGHT OF THE WORLD IS NOT ABOUT CHRISTMAS, BUT RATHER YAHUSHA BEING THE LIVING WORD, TEACHING TORAH

Beth Lekem (house of bread). Shabuoth was being observed at Acts 2, a wedding anniversary of the marriage between Yahuah & Yisharal that occurred at Sinai, the giving of the Living Words, or Covenant. The marriage Covenant is spoken of by Stephen at Acts 7. He uttered the Name aloud and was stoned for it. Hebrew roots are uniform in the reader's mind in this translation.

"*Besorah*" is equivalent to the Greek word *EUANGELION* (G2098) which became transformed into a newly created word, *GOSPEL* (god+spel). When you read the word "gospel" in your old versions, it is really the Hebrew word **besorah**: *message*. The objective is to make this the best translation for **the next generation of Yahusha's followers**. You will be delighted to see the new improvements, such as how "**the apple of My eye**" is rendered. The world inherited this from the KJV.

The Hebrew word, *ishon* (little-man of the eye), is not a fruit, or "*apple*." This was first used in the KJV, 1611.

The Hebrew idiom can be rendered several ways, but *apple* would not be the most appropriate. It relates to the popularized myth that the **fruit of temptation** was an apple. The KJV was made by Anglican Catholics using the Latin Vulgate. No apples are involved in either case.

The abstract meaning, rather than the literal meaning, points to the object of our **affections**, something highly valued we fix our attention on.

The BYNV translates this Hebrew word **treasure** as informed by the context (surrounding sentences).

This idea of *treasure* illuminates the words of Yahusha, and how it relates to the "ishon," or little man of the eye:
"For where your **treasure** is, there your **heart** shall be also. [see Proverbs 7:1,2 below] "The lamp of the body is the **eye**. If therefore your eye is good, all your body shall be enlightened." Mt. 6:21

You can see that Yahusha was involved in this translation, just from making this connection between eye, treasure, and the Hebrew word ishon.

"My son, guard my words, And treasure up My commands with you. Guard my commands and live, And My Torah as the treasure of your eye."

Are we the apple, or the treasure of His eye? Does your version copy the Anglican Catholic KJV, A direct translation from the Catholic Latin Vulgate?

Google: BYNV

You can get the Kindle Version in seconds:

amazon.com

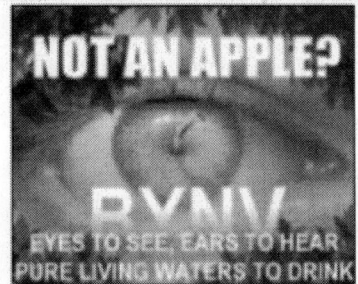

The soft cover is a 6" x 9" paperback. The deluxe cover edition has smyth-sewn pages and a white ribbon. Available by phone or online ordering:

TORAHZONE.NET

 DOWNLOAD THIS ARTICLE AND DOZENS OF OTHERS HERE:
lamblegacyfoundation.com

(BYNV tract, page 2 of 4)

The four photos above are from a downloadable PDF you can obtain for free at www.torahzone.net

1 Korinthians 13:1-13 describes love for us:
"If I speak with the tongues of men and of messengers, but do not have love, I have become as sounding brass or a clanging cymbal. And if I have prophecy, and know all secrets and all knowledge, and if I have all belief, so as to remove mountains, but do not have love, I am none at all. And if I give out all my possessions to feed the poor, and if I give my body to be burned, but do not have love, I am not profited at all. Love is patient, is kind, love does not envy, love does not boast, is not puffed up, does not behave indecently, does not seek its own, is not provoked, reckons not the evil, does not rejoice over the disobedience, but rejoices in the truth, it covers all, believes all, expects all, endures all. Love never fails. And whether there be prophecies, they shall be inactive; or tongues, they shall cease; or knowledge, it shall be inactive. For we know in part and we prophesy in part. But when that which is perfect has come, then that which is in part shall be inactive. When I was a child, I spoke as a child, I thought as a child, I reasoned as a child. But when I became a man, I did away with childish things. For now we see in a mirror, dimly, but then face to face. Now I know in part, but then I shall know, as I also have been known. And now belief, expectation, and love remain – these 3. But the greatest of these is love."
"The heaven and the arets shall pass away, but My Words shall by no means pass away." Mt. 24:35 – BYNV

"Do not think that I came to destroy the Turah or the Prophets. I did not come to destroy but to complete. For truly, I say to you, till the heaven and the arets pass away, one yod or one tittle shall by no means pass from the Turah till all be done. Whoever, then, breaks one of the least of these commands, and teaches men so, shall be called least in the reign of the shamayim; but whoever does and teaches them, he shall be called great in the reign of the shamayim." Mt. 5:17-19 BYNV

Teach all nations the Name, and to obey all we were commanded to obey. The traditions of men have been inherited from our fathers, and are futility. The Torah has been abandoned, and the way of Truth has been considered to be evil (2 Peter 2:2). If we abide in Yahusha's Word, we are truly His followers.

He said, **"I am the Vine, you are the Natsarim."** Yahuah is Yahusha, and the Natsarim are saying,

"Baruk haba bashem Yahuah."

If you have learned anything helpful from this book, please check out my author's page at amazon.com:

LETTER CHART

	HEBREW	ARAMAIC			GREEK		LATIN
alef	𐤀	א	1	ox	alpha	A	A
beth	𐤁	ב	2	house	beta	B	B
gimel	𐤂	ג	3	camel	gamma	Γ	G
daleth	𐤃	ד	4	door	delta	Δ	D
hay	𐤄	ה	5	window	hoi	H	H
uau	𐤅	ו	6	hook	**upsilon**	Y	U
zayin	𐤆	ז	7	weapon	zeta	Z	Z
heth	𐤇	ח	8	fence	(h)eta	H	CH
teth	𐤈	ט	9	winding	theta	Θ	T
yod	𐤉	׳	10	hand	iota	I	Y
kaph	𐤊	כ	20	bent hand	kappa	K	K
lamed	𐤋	ל	30	goad	lambda	Λ	L
mem	𐤌	מ	40	water	mu	M	M
nun	𐤍	נ	50	fish	nu	N	N
samek	𐤎	ס	60	prop	xei	Ξ	S
ayin	𐤏	ע	70	eye	**omega**	Ω	E/A
pe	𐤐	פ	80	mouth	pei	Π	P
tsadee	𐤑	צ	90	hook	zeta	Z	TS
koph	𐤒	ק	100	needle eye	chi	X	Q
resh	𐤓	ר	200	head	rho	P	R
shin	𐤔	ש	300	tooth	sigma	Σ	SH
tau	𐤕	ת	400	mark	tau	T	T

Made in the USA
Lexington, KY
13 November 2019